This book is

D1135271

NEW CENTURY READERS

A Northern Childhood

George Layton

Notes: Esther Menon

Longman

Edinburgh Gate
Harlow, Essex

Pearson Education Limited
Edinburgh Gate
Harlow
Essex
CM20 2JE
England

Contents

Introduction

An interview with George Layton

Interviewer: Were these stories closely based on your own childhood or did you change some of the incidents?

George Layton: My parents were refugees from Austria and I was the first member of the family to be born in England, so you can see that my home background was very different from that of the boy in the stories. The central incidents in the stories were all things that I experienced growing up in Bradford but I expanded and developed them. For instance, in 'The Fib', the Bobby Charlton character was actually me. I was making a presentation at the Town Hall when I saw my nephew in the crowd and asked him to come and have some tea in the Lord Mayor's parlour, and that incident gave me the idea for the story.

Interviewer: Why is the narrator never referred to by his name and why is his dad never mentioned?

George Layton: It was just a style that developed. I think that it leaves it open to the reader to decide who the boy is or to put themself in his place. In the same way I left the missing father as an open question. Is the boy illegitimate, is the mother a widow? You can decide for yourself.

Interviewer: Did you deliberately try to make the language sound as if a child is telling the story? Do you think that this is one of the features that make the stories popular with children?

George Layton: I certainly remembered the way I spoke as a child but I did not deliberately set out to make it sound childlike. You must also remember that I originally wrote the stories for an adult audience and perhaps that is one reason why children like them – because I am not talking down to them.

Interviewer: Why do girls play such a small part in the stories?

George Layton: In the earlier stories it is because the boy is only nine or 10 and at that age things like bikes and conkers are more important to him. As he gets older, girls play a bigger part in his life and certainly 'The Foursome' is all about girls.

Interviewer: Why did you decide on a series of short stories rather than one novel containing all the incidents?

George Layton: It was accidental. I wrote the first story to read as an audition piece for *Woman's Hour* and the BBC liked it and said that they would be interested if I had any more. I wrote them over a number of years and the length was determined by the fact that they had to fit a twenty-minute slot. They do stand on their own but they could be linked to form one long narrative. I would like to write a novel but the pressures of writing scripts for TV and my acting commitments do not leave me a great deal of time.

Interviewer: Did the fact that the stories were originally written to be broadcast on the radio make any difference to the way that you wrote them?

George Layton: The style is very direct because they were written to be read out loud. You have to let the listener know who is speaking and what is happening without going into explanations all the time. You will notice that when someone speaks it never says 'he said' or 'she replied' – it shouldn't be necessary.

Interviewer: These stories are set in the north of England in the 1950s. Do you ever go back there now? Has it changed a lot?

George Layton: No one in my family lives in Bradford now but I do occasionally go back for a visit. It has changed a lot and it saddens me to see how much of its individuality has been lost with the demolition of many of the fine Victorian buildings. The town may have lost its heart but the people have not and I have a great deal of affection for them. I still feel that I am a Northerner at heart.

Interviewer: You use a number of dialect words and expressions. Now that you have lived in London for a long time do you find that you still use as many in your own speech?

George Layton: As an actor I have to speak in many different dialects and with many different accents. I still have a northern accent but I don't naturally use dialect forms now although I can still remember expressions from my childhood. When I wrote the stories I deliberately meant them to sound different from the bland, middle-class language that you tended to hear on the radio then.

Interviewer: Are you planning to write any more stories about Norbert, Barry, Tony and the rest?

George Layton: I have written another collection called 'The Swap' (published by Macmillan). I am pleased that the stories are still relevant to kids. Although they are about events that happened quite a long time ago they don't seem to be regarded as period pieces. In all the years that I have been reading them to groups of children, not one has asked me who Wilfred Pickles is!

Interviewer: Have you been influenced by any other writers?

George Layton: The best piece of advice that I was given was by Stan Barstow. I was acting in Alfred Bradley's radio adaptation of Barstow's short story 'The Desperadoes' and he told me that I should write my stories in the first person, and it has certainly worked for me.

George Layton was interviewed by David Meaden.

Setting the scene

As the title of the book suggests, *A Northern Childhood* is about a child growing up in the north of England. Although it is set in the 1950s, the experiences, people and incidents it describes are realistic and familiar to most of us, portraying a boy's life at home and at school. In fact, much that George Layton describes is based on his own experience, growing up in Bradford in the 1950s. The 10 stories describe incidents in the life of a boy, tracing his development from a child to a teenager; from primary school through to his first job. The stories are told from the perspective of this narrator, and we follow his childhood experiences and observe his reactions. They are often lively and humorous, and sometimes touching and sad.

Main characters

The main character in the stories is the narrator, who describes memorable incidents in his life that are common to most of us: bonfire night, school camp, holidays, meeting someone famous, first dates and exams. Since the stories are told in the first person, we are able to empathise with the narrator. His inexperience of life often leads him to make foolish decisions, and we are able to laugh and share his worries at the possible consequences of his actions.

He is brought up by his mother, who appears to be a strong influence on his life, right through to the final story that ends with the line 'My mum's very proud of me'. Despite the fact that by this point the narrator has left school and is a working adult, his mother's opinion still matters to him. She brings him up on her own, with apparently little money; this sometimes prevents him from being 'one of the gang' when he can't have the right clothes or do the things they do. We never learn what happened to his father, whether he is dead or lives elsewhere. The boy obviously has a little of his mother's dogged determination, and at times as he grows up he ignores her advice and, consequently, gets into

4

trouble – from making a jelly made of aspic to stealing someone else's balaclava to be like his friends.

As the stories develop we get to know the characters of the other boys from school. Those we hear most about are Tony Wainwright who walks to school with the narrator each morning and the rather dominating Barry who is the oldest of the three friends. We also meet the wild and outrageous Norbert Lightowler and the two bullies Gordon Barraclough and Arthur Boocock.

The other characters in school are the teachers. George Layton gives us realistically varied portrayals of these adults: strict Mr Melrose, firm but kind Miss Taylor and Mr Garnett to whom the narrator feels he can talk. Through some of the more aggressive teachers, such as Mr Melrose, we can see the differences between school in the 1950s and the present day.

Main themes

The main focus of *A Northern Childhood* is growing up, and the themes and issues which run through the stories are anchored in this. As the narrator matures we can trace his both changing and unchanging reactions to people and situations. The issue of girls is one that inevitably changes as we move from the early stories where the narrator regards girls as 'daft' to the later ones where he thinks about Janis Webster and 'couldn't get her out of [his] mind'. The theme of bullying is one where we can also trace a change in our narrator's reactions, as in 'The Gang-hut' he submits to Barry's bullying, but later, in 'The Mile', he is able to challenge the bully Arthur Boocock.

Relationships at home and school are central to the novel and the conflicting demands of teachers, friends and family often cause tension as the narrator grows up. Despite the narrator's growing independence as the stories progress, the influence of his mother remains strong. The importance of friends is also constant

5

throughout the stories and the issue of peer pressure is one that is addressed frequently, from the importance of being in a boys' gang in the early stories to following friends' fashion and behaviour with girls in 'The Foursome'.

Language and style

The stories are written in an informal style as George Layton reflects the youthful perspective of his narrator. As the stories were written for radio there is little description of setting and atmosphere. Much of the narrative is reflected in dialogue and we learn about characters and their relationships through what they say. This dialogue realistically conveys some of the accent and dialect of the north of England.

A Northern Childhood

Notes on The Balaclava Story

We are introduced to the narrator and meet several of the characters that are developed throughout *A Northern Childhood*. We start to understand the narrator's character and his relationships with others.

What do you think?
Consider the narrator's feelings about his friends, teacher and mother. How do these lead to conflicting emotions and create worry in his life?

Questions
1. How does the first sentence of the story make you want to read on?
2. Give three reasons why the narrator wants a balaclava. Find evidence in the author's words to back up your answers.
3. Look at page 11: 'Why wouldn't *my mum* buy *me* a *balaclava*?' Why does the author use italics? Read the sentence aloud. Change the meaning of the sentence by italicising other words instead.
4. Pause at page 15: 'I'd have to get rid of the blooming thing as fast as I could.' What could happen next?
5. Write two sentences explaining what the last line of the story reveals.

Further activities
1. 'I put the curse of the middle finger on her.' Poetry is often used for charms and curses, since it uses words in a powerful way. For example, find and compare the charm spoken by the fairies to protect Titania in *A Midsummer Night's Dream*: "You spotted snakes ...", and the witches' from *Macbeth*: "Double, double, toil and trouble".

   Make up your own charm, for example to cure someone of an illness or a curse to make it rain. Think carefully about the language and images you choose and how they fit in with the purpose of your charm.

2. Find out about *Robinson Crusoe*. Who wrote this famous book and what is it about?

8

The Balaclava Story

Tony and Barry both had one. I reckon half the kids in our class had one. But I didn't. My mum wouldn't even listen to me.

'You're not having a balaclava! What do you want a balaclava for in the middle of summer?'

I must've told her about ten times why I wanted a balaclava.

'I want one so's I can join the Balaclava Boys …'

'Go and wash your hands for tea, and don't be so silly.'

She turned away from me to lay the table, so I put the curse of the middle finger on her. This was pointing both your middle fingers at somebody when they weren't looking – Tony had started it when Miss Taylor gave him a hundred lines for flicking paper pellets at Jennifer Greenwood. He had to write out a hundred times:

'I must not fire missiles because it is dangerous and liable to cause damage to someone's eye.'

Tony tried to tell Miss Taylor that he hadn't fired a missile, he'd just flicked a paper pellet, but she threw a piece of chalk at him and told him to shut up.

'Don't just stand there – wash your hands.'

'Eh?'

'Don't say "eh", say "pardon".'

'What?'

'Just hurry up, and make sure the dirt comes off in the water, and not on the towel, do you hear?'

Ooh, my mum. She didn't half go on sometimes.

9

'I don't know what you get up to at school. How do you get so dirty?'

I knew exactly the kind of balaclava I wanted. One just like Tony's – a sort of yellowy-brown. His dad had given it to him 'cos of his ear-ache. Mind you, he didn't like wearing it at first. At school he'd give it to Barry to wear and got it back before home-time. But, all the other lads started asking if they could have a wear of it, so Tony took it back and said from then on nobody but him could wear it – not even Barry. Barry told him he wasn't bothered 'cos he was going to get a balaclava of his own – and so did some of the other lads – and that's how it started – the Balaclava Boys.

It wasn't a gang really. I mean they didn't have meetings or anything like that. They just went around together wearing their balaclavas, and if you didn't have one you couldn't go around with them. Tony and Barry were my best friends, but 'cos I didn't have a balaclava, they wouldn't let me go round with them. I tried.

'Aw, go on Barry, let us walk round with you.'

'No, you can't. You're not a Balaclava Boy.'

'Aw, go on.'

'No.'

'Please.'

I don't know why I wanted to walk round with them anyway. All they did was wander up and down the play-ground dressed in their rotten balaclavas. It was daft.

'Go on Barry, be a sport.'

'I've told you. You're not a Balaclava Boy. You've got to have a balaclava. If you get one, you can join.'

'But I can't, Barry. My mum won't let me have one.'

'Hard luck.'

'You're rotten.'

Then he went off with the others. I wasn't half fed-up. All my friends were in the Balaclava Boys. All the lads in my class except me. Wasn't fair. The bell went for the next lesson – ooh heck, handicraft with the Miseryguts Garnett – then it was home-time. All the Balaclava Boys were going in and I followed them.

'Hey Tony – do you want to go down the woods after school?'

'No – I'm going round with the Balaclava Boys.'

'Oh.'

Blooming Balaclava Boys. Why wouldn't *my mum* buy *me* a *balaclava*. Didn't she realise that I was losing all my friends – and just 'cos she wouldn't buy me one.

'Eh, Tony, we can go goose-gogging – you know by those super gooseberry bushes at the other end of the woods.'

'I've told you, I can't.'

'Yes, I know, but I thought you might want to go goose-gogging.'

'Well, I would – but I can't.'

I wondered if Barry would be going as well.

'Is Barry going round with the Balaclava Boys an' all?'

'Course he is.'

'Oh.'

11

Blooming balaclavas. I wish they'd never been invented.

'Why won't your mum get you one?'

'I don't know. She says it's daft wearing a balaclava in the middle of summer. She won't let me have one.'

'I found mine at home up in our attic.'

Tony unwrapped some chewing-gum and asked me if I wanted a piece.

'No thanks.' I'd've only had to wrap it in my handkerchief once we got in the classroom. You couldn't get away with anything with Mr Garnett.

'Hey, maybe you could find one in your attic.'

For a minute I wasn't sure what he was talking about.

'Find what?'

'A balaclava.'

'No, we haven't even got an attic.'

I didn't half find handicraft class boring.

All that mucking about with compasses and rulers. Or else it was weaving – and you got all tangled up with balls of wool. I was just no good at handicraft and Mr Garnett agreed with me. Today was worse than ever. We were painting pictures and we had to call it 'My favourite story'. Tony was painting *Noddy in Toyland*. I told him he'd get into trouble.

'Garnett'll do you.'

'Why – it's my favourite story.'

'Yes, but I don't think he'll believe you.

Tony looked ever so hurt.

'But honest. It's my favourite story. Anyway what are you doing?'

He leaned over to have a look at my favourite story. 'Have you read it, Tony?'

'I don't know. What is it?'

'It's *Robinson Crusoe* – what do you think it is?'

He just looked at my painting.

'Oh, I see it now. Oh yes, I get it now. I couldn't make it out for a minute. Oh yes, there's Man Friday behind him.'

'Get your finger off – it's still wet. And that isn't Man Friday, it's a coconut tree. And you've smudged it.'

We were using some stuff called poster paint, and I got covered in it. I was getting it everywhere, so I asked Mr Garnett if I could go for a wash. He gets annoyed when you ask to be excused, but he could see I'd got it all over my hands, so he said I could go, but told me to be quick.

The wash-basins were in the boys' cloakroom just outside the main hall. I got most of the paint off and as I was drying my hands that's when it happened. I don't know what came over me. As soon as I saw that balaclava lying there on the floor, I decided to pinch it. I couldn't help it. I just knew that this was my only chance. I've never pinched anything before – I don't think I have, but I didn't think of this as …well … I don't even like saying it – but …well stealing. I just did it.

I picked it up, went to my coat, and put it in the pocket. At least I tried to put it in the pocket but it bulged out, so I pushed it down the inside of the sleeve. My head was throbbing, and even though I'd just dried my hands, they were all wet from sweating. If only I'd thought a bit first. But it all happened so quickly. I went back to the classroom, and as I was going in I began to realise what I'd done. I'd *stolen* a balaclava. I didn't even know whose it was, but as I stood in the doorway I couldn't believe I'd done it. If only I could go back – in fact I thought I would but then Mr Garnett told me to hurry up and sit down. As I was going back to my desk I felt as if all the lads knew what I'd done. How could they? Maybe somebody had seen me. No! Yes! How *could* they? They could. Course they couldn't. No, course not. What if they did though? Oh heck.

I thought home-time would never come but when the bell did ring I got out as quick as I could. I was going to put the balaclava back before anybody noticed; but as I got to the cloakroom I heard Norbert Lightowler shout out that someone had pinched his balaclava. Nobody took much notice, thank goodness, and I heard Tony say to him that he'd most likely lost it. Norbert said he hadn't but he went off to make sure it wasn't in the classroom.

I tried to be all casual and took my coat, but I didn't dare put it on in case the balaclava popped out of the sleeve. I said tarah to Tony.

'Tarah Tony, see you tomorrow.'

'Yeh, tarah.'

Oh, it was good to get out in the open air. I couldn't wait to get home and get rid of that blooming balaclava. Why had I gone and done a stupid thing like that? Norbert Lightowler was sure to report it to the Headmaster, and there'd be an announcement about it at morning assembly and the culprit would be asked to own up. I was running home as fast as I could. I wanted to stop and take out the balaclava and chuck it away, but I didn't dare. The faster I ran, the faster my head was filled with thoughts. I could give it back to Norbert. You know, say I'd taken it by mistake. No, he'd never believe me. None of the lads would believe me. Everybody knew how much I wanted to be a Balaclava Boy. I'd have to get rid of the blooming thing as fast as I could.

My mum wasn't back from work when I got home, thank goodness, so as soon as I shut the front door, I put my hand down the sleeve of my coat for the balaclava. There was nothing there. That was funny, I was sure I'd put it down that sleeve. I tried down the other sleeve, and there was still nothing there. Maybe I'd got the wrong coat – no, it was my coat all right. Oh, blimey, I must've lost it while I was running home. I was glad in a way. I was going to have to get rid of it – now it was gone. I only hoped nobody had seen it drop out, but, oh, I was glad to be rid of it. Mind you, I was dreading going to school next morning. Norbert'll have probably reported it by now. Well, I wasn't going to own up. I didn't mind, the cane – it wasn't that – but if you owned, up, you had to go up on the stage in front of the whole school. Well I was going to forget about it now – and nobody would ever know that I'd pinched that blooming lousy balaclava.

I started to do my homework, but I couldn't concentrate. I kept thinking about assembly next morning. What if I went all red and everybody else noticed? They'd know I'd pinched it then. I tried to think about other things – nice things. I thought about bed. I just wanted to go to sleep. To go to bed and sleep. Then I thought about my mum. What she'd say if she knew I'd been stealing – but I still couldn't forget about assembly next day. I went into the kitchen and peeled some potatoes for my mum. She was ever so pleased when she came in from work and said I must've known she'd brought me a present.

'Oh, thanks. What've you got me?'

She gave me a paper bag and when I opened it I couldn't believe my eyes – a blooming balaclava.

'There you are, now you won't be left out and you can stop making my life a misery.'

'Thanks Mum.'

If only my mum knew she was making *my* life a misery. The balaclava she'd bought me was just like the one I'd pinched. I felt sick – I didn't want it. I couldn't wear it now. If I did, everybody would say it was Norbert Lightowler's. Even if they didn't, I just couldn't wear it. I wouldn't feel it was mine. I had to get rid of it. I went outside and put it down the lavatory. I had to pull the chain three times before it went away. It's a good job we've got an outside lavatory or else my mum would have wondered what was wrong with me.

I could hardly eat my tea.

'What's wrong with you? Aren't you hungry?'

'No, not much.'

'What've you been eating? You've been eating sweets, haven't you?'

'No, I don't feel hungry.'

'Don't you feel well?'

'I'm all right.'

I wasn't, I felt terrible. I told my mum I was going upstairs to work on my model aeroplane.

'Well, it's my bingo night, so make yourself some cocoa before you go to bed.'

I went upstairs to bed, and after a while I fell asleep. The last thing I remember, was a big balaclava – with a smiling face – and it was the headmaster's face.

I was scared stiff when I went to school next morning. In assembly it seemed different. All the boys were looking at me. Norbert Lightowler pushed past and didn't say anything. When prayers finished I just stood there waiting for the Headmaster to ask for the culprit to own up – but he was talking about the school fete. And then he said he had something very important to announce – and I could feel myself going red. My ears were burning like anything and I was going hot and cold both at the same time.

'I'm very pleased to announce that the school football team has won the inter-league cup ...'

And that was the end of assembly, except that we were told to go and play in the school-yard until we were all called in, because there was a teachers' meeting. I couldn't understand why I hadn't been found out yet, but I still didn't feel any better – I'd probably be called to the Headmaster's room later on.

I went out into the yard. Everybody was happy 'cos we were having extra playtime. I could see all the Balaclava Boys going round together – and then I saw Norbert Lightowler was one of them. I couldn't be sure it was Norbert 'cos he had a balaclava on, so I had to go up close to him. Yes, it was Norbert – he must have bought a new balaclava that morning.

'Have you bought a new one then, Norbert?'

'Y'what?'

'You've bought a new balaclava, have you?'

'What are you talking about?'

'Your balaclava. You've got a new balaclava, haven't you?'

'No, I never lost it, at all. Some fool had shoved it down the sleeve of my raincoat.'

Notes on The Christmas Party

The settings of this story remain the same as the first, school and home. Like 'The Balaclava Story' we move from school to home and then back to school. Yet again, it is the tension and difference between school and home that create worry for the narrator. His actions to resolve this lead once again to deceit and chaos in his life.

What do you think?
As you read through the story, pick out clues that show this is an early story in the narrator's life. How can you tell he is young and at junior school?

Questions
1. Identify the four settings that are used in this story.
2. What excites the narrator about Christmas? How does this differ from what his teacher thinks about it?
3. From the first three pages, what can you tell about the type of teacher Miss Taylor is? Find evidence to prove your answers. Would you have liked her as your junior school teacher?
4. Read aloud the sentence on pages 25–6 that begins: 'And then Miss Taylor explained that all these others are Father Christmas's brothers'. What do you notice about the punctuation?

Further activity
Start to make a list of the familiar phrases that teachers or parents use. You will find examples in the mother's speech in this story, such as '"Do you know what time it is?"' and '"If I hear another word out of you"'. Turn your list into a poem entitled 'Parents' sayings' or 'Teachers' sayings'. You might like to perform it to the class, or make a poster poem on sugar paper incorporating ideas from other people in your class. If possible, read Michael Rosens' poem, called 'Chivy', which uses this idea.

The Christmas Party

Our classroom looked smashing. Lots of silver tinsel and crepe paper and lanterns. *We'd* made the lanterns, but Miss Taylor had bought the rest herself, out of her own money. Oh, only today and tomorrow and then we break up. Mind you, if school was like this all the time, I wouldn't be bothered about breaking up. Putting up Christmas decorations and playing games – much better than doing writing and spelling any day. I watched the snow coming down outside. Smashing! More sliding tomorrow. I love Christmas. I wish it was more than once a year. Miss Taylor started tapping on the blackboard with a piece of chalk. Everybody was talking and she kept on tapping 'till the only person you could hear was Norbert Lightowler.

'Look, if I get a six and land on you, you get knocked off and I still get another go!'

The whole class was looking at him.

'Look, when Colin got a six, he landed on *me* and *he* got another …!'

Suddenly he realised that he was the only one talking and he started going red.

'Thank you, Norbert, I think we all know the rules of Ludo.'

Miss Taylor can be right sarcastic sometimes. Everybody laughed. Even Miss Taylor smiled.

'Now, since it is getting so noisy, we're going to stop these games and do some work.'

Everybody groaned and Tony and me booed – quietly so Miss Taylor couldn't hear. She hates people that boo. She says people who boo are cowards.

'Who is that booing?'

We must have been booing louder than we thought.

'Who is that booing?'

Miss Taylor looked at Tony. I looked at Tony. They both looked at me. I put my hand up.

'It was me, Miss.'

Tony put his hand up.

'It was me an' all, Miss.'

She looked at us.

'You both know what I think of booing, don't you?'

We nodded.

'Yes, Miss.'

'Yes, Miss.'

'Don't ever let me hear it again.'

We shook our heads.

'No, Miss.'

'No, Miss.'

She turned to the class.

'Now, the work I have in mind is discussion work.'

Everybody groaned again – except me and Tony.

'I thought we'd discuss tomorrow's Christmas party!'

We all cheered and Miss Taylor smiled. We have a Christmas party every year, the whole school together in the main hall. Each class has its own table and we all bring the food from home.

22

'Now, does everybody know what they're bringing from home for the party tomorrow?'

I knew. I was bringing a jelly. I put my hand up.

'I'm bringing a jelly, Miss!'

Everybody started shouting at once and Miss Taylor moved her hands about to calm us down.

'All right, all right, one at a time. Don't get excited. Jennifer Greenwood, what are you bringing?'

Jennifer Greenwood was sitting in the back row next to Valerie Burns. She wriggled her shoulders and rolled her head about and looked down. She always does that when she's asked a question. She's daft is Jennifer Greenwood.

'C'mon Jennifer, what are you bringing for tomorrow?'

She put her hand up.

'Please, Miss, I'm bringing a custard trifle, Miss.'

Norbert Lightowler pulled his mouth into a funny shape and pretended to be sick.

'Ugh, I hate custard. I'm not gonna have any of that!'

Everybody laughed, except Miss Taylor.

'Well, Norbert – if I was Jennifer I wouldn't dream of giving you any. Right Jennifer?'

Jennifer just rolled her head about and giggled with Valerie Burns. Norbert was looking down at his desk.

'And Norbert, what are you bringing tomorrow?'

'Polony sandwiches, Miss, my mum's making 'em, and a bottle of mixed pickles, Miss, home-made!'

Miss Taylor said that would be lovely, and carried on asking right round the class. Tony said that he was bringing a Christmas cake. I was bringing the jelly that my mum was going to make, and Colin Wilkinson was bringing some currant buns. Valerie Burns said she was bringing some lemon-curd tarts, and Freda Holdsworth called her a spiteful cat 'cos *she* was bringing the lemon-curd tarts, and Valerie Burns *knew* she was bringing lemon-curd tarts 'cos she'd told her and she was a blooming copy-cat. Anyway Miss Taylor calmed her down by saying that it was a good job they were both bringing lemon-curd tarts, because then there would be enough for everybody, and everybody would want one, wouldn't they? And she asked everybody who would want a lemon-curd tart to put their hands up, and everybody put their hands up. Even I put my hand up and I hate lemon-curd. Well, it *was* Christmas.

After everybody had told Miss Taylor what they were bringing, she said that there'd be enough for the whole school, never mind just our class, but we should remember that Christmas isn't just for eating and parties, and she asked Tony what the most important thing about Christmas is.

'Presents, Miss!'

'No Tony, not presents. Christmas is when the baby Jesus was born, and that is the most important thing, and when you're all enjoying your presents and parties this year, you must all remember that. Will you all promise me?'

Everybody promised that they'd remember Jesus and then Miss Taylor started asking us all how we were going to spend Christmas. Freda Holdsworth said she was going to Bridlington on Christmas Eve to stay with her cousin, and on Christmas Eve they'd both put their stockings up for Father Christmas, but before they'd go to bed, they'd leave a glass of milk and some biscuits for him in case he's hungry. Norbert Lightowler said that that's daft 'cos there's no such thing as Father Christmas. Some of the others agreed, but most of 'em said course there is. I just wasn't sure. What I can't understand is, that if there *is* a Father Christmas, how does he get round everybody in one night? I mean the presents must come from somewhere, but how can he do it all by himself? And Norbert said how can there be only *one* Father Christmas, when he'd seen *two* down in town in Baldwin Street and another outside the fish market, and Neville Bastow said he'd seen one in Dickenson's (that's a big department store). Well, what about the one my mum had taken me to see at the Co-op. He'd promised to bring me a three-wheeler.

'Please Miss, there's one at the Co-op an' all. He's promised to bring me a three-wheeler.'

And then Miss Taylor explained that all these others are Father Christmas's brothers and relations who help him out 'cos he's so busy and Freda Holdsworth said Miss Taylor was right, and Norbert said he'd never thought of that, but that Paul Hopwood, he's in 2B, had told him that Father Christmas is just his dad dressed up, and I said that that's daft and it couldn't be 'cos Father Christmas comes to our house every year and I haven't got a dad,

25

and Miss Taylor said that if those who didn't believe in Father Christmas didn't get any presents, they'd only have themselves to blame, and I agreed! Then she asked me what I'd be doing on Christmas day.

'Well, Miss, when I wake up in the morning, I'll look round and see what presents I've got, and I'll play with them and I'll empty my stocking, and usually there are some sweets so I'll eat them, and when I've played a bit more I'll go and wake my mum up and show her what I've got, and then I'll wake my Auntie Doreen – she always stays with us every Christmas; and then after breakfast I'll play a bit more, and then we'll have us Christmas dinner, and then we'll go to my grandad's and I'll play a bit more there, and then I'll go home to bed, and that'll be the end!'

Miss Taylor said that all sounded very nice and she hoped everybody would have such a nice Christmas, but she was surprised I wasn't going to Church. Well, I told her that there wouldn't really be time 'cos my grandad likes us to be there early to hear Wilfred Pickles on the wireless visiting a hospital, and to listen to the Queen talking, and then the bell went for home-time and Miss Taylor said we could all go quietly and told us not to forget our stuff for the party.

I went with Tony to get our coats from the cloakroom. Everybody was talking about the party and Barry was there shouting out that their class was going to have the best table 'cos their teacher had made them a Christmas pudding with money in it! I told him that was nothing

26

'cos Miss Taylor had given everybody in our class sixpence, but he didn't believe me.

'Gerraway, you bloomin' fibber.'

'She did, didn't she Tony?'

Tony shook his head.

'Did she heckers-like – she wouldn't give 'owt away.'

Huh! You'd think Tony'd've helped me kid Barry along.

'Well, she bought all our Christmas decorations for the classroom ...' and I went to get my coat. I took my gloves out of my pocket and they were still soaking wet from snow-balling at playtime, so I thought I'd put them on the pipes to dry.

'Hey Tony, my gloves are still sodden.'

'Well put 'em on the pipes.'

'Yeh, that's a good idea.'

While they dried I sat on the pipes. Ooh, it was lovely and warm. There's a window above the basins and I could see the snow was still coming down – really thick now.

'Hey, it isn't half going to be deep tomorrow.'

Everybody had gone now except for Barry, Tony and me. Tony was standing on the basins looking out of the window and Barry was doing up his coat – it has a hood on it. I wish I had one like it. I could see through the door into the main hall where the Christmas tree was. It looked lovely. Ever so big. It was nearly up to the ceiling.

'Hey, isn't it a big Christmas tree?' Tony jumped down from the basin and came over to where I was sitting.

'Yeh. It's smashing. All them coloured balls. Isn't it lovely, eh Barry?'

Barry came over.

'Not bad. C'mon you two, let's get going, eh?'

'Just a sec', let's see if my gloves are dry.'

They weren't really but I put 'em on. As I was fastening my coat up Barry said how about going carol-singing to get a bit of money.

Tony was quite keen, but I didn't know. I mean my mum'd be expecting me home round about now…

'I suppose *you* can't come 'cos your mum'll be cross with you …as usual!'

Huh. It's all right for Barry. His mum and dad aren't bothered where he goes.

'Course I'll come. Where do you want to go?'

Barry said down near the woods where the posh live, but Tony said it was useless there 'cos they never gave you nowt. So we decided to go round Belgrave Road way, where it's only *quite* posh. It takes about ten minutes to get to Belgrave Road from our school and on the way we argued about which carols to sing. I wanted *Away in a Manger* but Barry wanted *O Come all Ye Faithful*.

'*Away in a Manger* isn't half as good as *O Come all Ye Faithful*, is it Tony?'

Tony shrugged his shoulders.

'I quite like *Once in Royal David's City*.'

In the end we decided to take it in turns to choose.

Belgrave Road's ever so long and we started at number three with *O Come all Ye Faithful*.

'O come all ye faithful, joyful and trium ...'

That was as far as we got. A bloke opened the door, gave us three-halfpence and told us to push off.

Tony was disgusted.

'That's a good start, halfpenny each.'

Barry told him to stop grumbling.

'It's better than nothing. C'mon.'

We went on to number five and Tony and Barry started quarrelling again 'cos Tony said it was his turn to choose, but Barry wanted his go again 'cos we'd only sung one line. So we did *O Come all Ye Faithful* again.

'Oh come all ye faithful, joyful and triumphant,

Oh...'

We didn't get any further this time neither. An old lady opened the door and said her mother was poorly so could we sing a bit quieter. We started once more but she stopped us again and said it was still just a little bit too loud and could we sing it quieter.

'O come all ye faithful, joyful and triumphant,

O come ye, o come ye to Beth-eth-lehem ...'

And we sang the whole thing like that, in whispers. We could hardly hear each other. I felt daft and started giggling and that set Tony and Barry off, but the old lady didn't seem to notice. She just stood there while we sang and when we finished she said thank you and gave us twopence each.

At the next house we sang *Once in Royal David's City* right through and then rang the doorbell – but nobody came. We missed number nine out 'cos it was empty and up for sale, and at number eleven we sang *Away in a Manger.*

We went right to the end of the road singing every carol we knew. We must've made about a pound between us by the time we got to the other end, and Barry said how about going back and doing the other side of the road. I was all for it, but I just happened to see St Chad's clock. Bloomin' heck! Twenty to nine! I couldn't believe it. I thought it'd be about half-past six, if that. Twenty to nine!

'Hey, I'd better get going. It's twenty to nine. My mum'll kill me!'

The other two said they were gonna do a bit more carol-singing, so they gave me my share of the money and I ran home as fast as I could. I took a short cut through the snicket behind the fish and chip shop and I got home in about five minutes. I could see my Mum standing outside the front door talking to Mrs Theabould, our next door neighbour. She saw me and walked towards me. I tried to act all calm as if it was only about half-past five or six o'clock.

'Hullo Mum, I've been carol-singing.'

She gave me a clout. She nearly knocked me over. Right on my freezing cold ear an' all.

'Get inside, you! I've been going mad with worry. Do you know what time it is? Nine o'clock. Get inside!'

She pushed me inside and I heard her thank Mrs Theabould and come in after me. I thought she was gonna give me another clout, but she just shouted at me, saying that I was lucky she didn't get the police out, and why didn't I tell her where I was? By this time I was crying my head off.

'But I was only bloomin' carol-singing.'

'I'll give you carol-singing. Get off to bed,' and she pushed me upstairs into my bedroom.

'But what about my jelly for tomorrer. Have you made it?'

I thought she was going to go mad.

'Jelly! I'll give you jelly. If you think I've nothing better to do than make jellies while you're out roaming the streets! Get to bed!'

'But I've told Miss Taylor I'm bringing a jelly. I've got to have one. Please, Mum.'

She just told me to wash my hands and face and get to bed.

'And if I hear another word out of you, you'll get such a good hiding, you'll wish you hadn't come home …' and she went downstairs.

I didn't dare say another word. What was I gonna do about my jelly? I had to bring one. I'd promised. There was only one thing for it. I'd have to make one myself. So I decided to wait 'till my mum went to bed, and then I'd go downstairs and make one. I don't know how I kept awake. I'm sure I nodded off once or twice, but after a while I heard my mum switch her light out, and when I'd given her enough time to get to sleep, I crept downstairs.

I've seen my mum make jellies tons of times and I knew you had to have boiling water, so I put the kettle on. I looked in the cupboard for a jelly and at first I thought I'd had it, but I found one and emptied it into a glass bowl. It was a funny jelly. Not like the ones my mum usually has. It was sort of like a powder. Still, it said jelly on the packet, so it was all right. A new flavour most likely. I poured the hot water into a bowl, closed the cupboard door, switched off the light, and took the jelly upstairs and I put it under my bed. I could hear my mum snoring so I knew I was all right, and I went to sleep.

Next thing I heard was my mum shouting from downstairs.

'C'mon, get up or you'll be late for school.'

I got up and pulled the jelly from under the bed. It had set lovely. All wobbly. But it was a bit of a funny colour – sort of yellowy-white. Still I'd got my jelly and that's what mattered. My mum didn't say much when I got downstairs. She just told me to eat my breakfast and get to school, so I did. When I finished I put my coat on and said tarah to my mum in the kitchen and went off. But first I sneaked upstairs and got my jelly and wrapped it in a piece of newspaper.

The first thing we had to do at school was to take what we'd brought for the party into the main hall and stick on a label with our name on it and leave it on our table. Norbert Lightowler was there with his polony sandwiches and mixed pickles. So was Neville Bastow. Neville Bastow said that my jelly was a bit funny-looking, but Norbert said he loved jelly more than anything else, and he could eat all the jellies in the world. Miss Taylor came along then and told us to take our coats off and go

32

to our classroom. The party wasn't starting till twelve o'clock, so in the morning we played games and sang carols and Miss Taylor read us a story.

Then we had a long playtime and we had a snowball fight with 2B, and I went on the slides 'till old Wilkie, that's the caretaker, came and put ashes on the ice. Then the bell went and we all had to go to our tables in the main hall. At every place was a Christmas cracker, and everybody had a streamer, but Mr Dyson, the Headmaster, said that we couldn't throw any streamers until we'd finished eating. I pulled my cracker with Tony and got a red paper hat and a pencil sharpener. Tony got a blue hat and a small magnifying glass. When everybody had pulled their crackers we said grace and started eating. I started with a sausage roll that Neville Bastow had brought, and a polony sandwich.

Miss Taylor had shared my jelly out in bowls and Jennifer Greenwood said it looked horrible and wasn't going to have any. So did Freda Holdsworth. But Norbert was already on his jelly and said it was lovely and he'd eat anybody else's. Tony started his jelly and spat it out.

'Ugh, it's horrible.'

I tasted mine, and it *was* horrible, but I forced it down.

'It's not that bad.'

Just then Tony said he could see my mum.

'Isn't that your mum over there?'

He pointed to the door. She was talking to Miss Taylor and they both came over.

'Your mother says you forgot your jelly this morning, here it is.'

Miss Taylor put a lovely red jelly on the table. It had bananas and cream on it, and bits of orange. My mum asked me where I'd got my jelly from. I told her I'd made it. I thought she'd be cross, but she and Miss Taylor just laughed and told us to enjoy ourselves, and then my mum went off. Everybody put their hands up for a portion of my mum's jelly – except Norbert.

'I don't want any of that. This is lovely.

What flavour is it?'

I told him it was a new flavour and I'd never heard of it before.

'Well, what's it called?'

'Aspic.'

'Y'what?'

'Aspic jelly – it's a new flavour!'

Norbert ate the whole thing and was sick afterwards, and everybody else had some of my mum's. It was a right good party.

Notes on The Long Walk

This story provides a contrasting mood to the others. It sensitively portrays the narrator's closeness to his grandfather. Unlike the breathless pace of the other stories, this is quite literally slower, and touching in its content. It shows that life is varied, and can be hard to understand.

What do you think?
As modern readers we are able to see many similarities between the 1950s and our time. Consider how George Layton shows us the links between the past and present: between the 1950s and Grandad's life and between the narrator and his grandfather.

Questions
1. Find two examples in the first paragraph of informal language that makes the reader feel involved.
2. What does the fact that the narrator wears his clogs show about him?
3. Identify the changes mentioned in the story that have taken place since the grandfather's younger days. Arrange them as a table with the headings *Then* and *Now*.
4. What clues does George Layton give us in the first three pages (to '"Are you all right, Grandad?"') that he is nearing the end of his life?
5. Having read the story, think of a new title which sums it up for you.

Further activities
1. George Layton uses dialogue, action and description to set up a warm and familiar atmosphere, e.g., 'grandad' and 'son' emphasise the close relationship between the two characters.
   - Select three quotes from the dialogue that reflect their close and loving relationship. Comment on the individual words and phrases and explain why you chose them.
   - Select three moments that reflect the cosy and loving atmosphere the writer tries to create. Comment on the individual words and phrases and explain why you chose them.

2. Imagine that you are the narrator of the story. Make an acrostic poem about the old man's character using the word 'grandad'.

The Long Walk

I loved it when my Grandad took me out – just me and him. I never knew when I was going out with him. It just happened every so often. My mum'd say to me, 'C'mon, get ready 'cos your grandad's coming to take you out. Get your clogs on.' – and that was the one thing that spoilt it – my clogs. Whenever my grandad took me out, I had to wear a pair of clogs that he'd given to me. Well he'd made them you see, that was his job before he retired, clog-maker. I didn't half make a noise when I was wearing them an' all. Blimey you could hear me a mile away. I hated those clogs.

'Aw, Mum, do I have to put my clogs on?'

'Now don't ask silly questions – go and get ready.'

'Aw, please ask Grandad if I can go without my clogs.'

'Do you want to go or don't you?'

My mum knew that I wanted to go.

'Course I want to go.'

'Then go and put your clogs on.'

'Oh, heck.'

Honest, I'd never ever seen anybody else wearing clogs. I wondered where my grandad would take me today. Last time I'd gone to the zoo with him – it was great. I was just about ready when I heard him knock at the front door. I knew it was my grandad, 'cos he always had his own special knock – everybody else used the bell. I could hear him downstairs – he was wearing clogs as well.

'I'm nearly ready, Grandad.'

I put on my windcheater that I'd been given last Christmas. It was maroon-coloured. My friend Tony had got one an' all only his was green, but I liked mine best – and I went downstairs.

'Hello, Grandad.'

My mum told me to give him a kiss.

'He's getting too big to give his old grandad a kiss, aren't you son?'

He always called me son.

'No, course not Grandad.'

He bent down so I could kiss him on his cheek. He was all bristly and it made me laugh.

'Ooh, Grandad, you haven't shaved today, have you?'

He was laughing as well. We were both laughing – we didn't really know why – and my mum started laughing. There we were, all three of us laughing at nothing at all.

'No son, I haven't shaved. But it doesn't matter today. It'll bother nobody else today. There's just the two of us.'

'Where are we going, Grandad, where are you taking us?'

He looked at me. His eyes were watering a bit and he wiped them with a dark blue hanky he always had in his top pocket.

'We're going on a walk – a special walk.'

He was almost whispering, as if he didn't want me mum to hear, bending down with his whiskery face next to mine.

'Where are we going, Grandad, where are we going? Is it a secret?'

'You'll see son, when we get there.'

He looked a bit sad for a minute, but then he smiled and put on his flat cap.

'C'mon son, let's get going.'

My mum gave us each a pack of sandwiches, and off we went. We must have looked a funny sight walking down the road together me and my grandad. Him dressed in his flat cap and thick overcoat and clogs. Me in my maroon windcheater and short grey trousers and clogs. But I was so happy. I didn't know where we were going and neither did anybody else. Only Grandad knew, and only I was going to find out.

'Are we walking all the way, Grandad?' He took such big strides that I was half walking and half running.

'No son, we'll get a trackless first to get out a bit.'

By 'trackless' he meant a bus, and I'd heard him say it so often that I never wondered why he said trackless.

'I'll show you where I used to go when I was a lad.'

We didn't have to wait long before a bus came, and we went upstairs and sat right at the front. Grandad was out of breath when we sat down.

'Are you all right, Grandad?'

'Oh, aye son. You get a better view up here.'

'Yes, Grandad, you do.'

Soon we were going through the 'posh part' where the snobs lived. This was on the other side of the park.

'At one time there were no roof on't top deck. That were before the trackless. Completely open it was – daft really.'

The conductor came round for our fares.

'One and t'lad to the basin.'

I'd never heard of the basin before. After my grandad had paid our fares I asked him what it was.

'What's the basin, Grandad?'

'That's where we start our walk.'

'What basin is it? Why is it called "basin"?'

'The canal basin – it's where the canal starts. You'll see.'

By now we were going through a brand new shopping centre.

'Hey, look Grandad, that's where that new bowling alley is. My friends Tony and Barry have been. They say it's smashing.'

Grandad looked out of the window.

'That's where I used to play cricket – a long time ago.'

'Where the bowling alley is?'

'That's right son, when they were fields. It's all changed now. Mind, where we're going for our walk – it's not changed there. No, it's just the same there.'

We heard the conductor shout 'basin'. 'C'mon, son, our stop, be careful now. Follow me.'

While we were going down the stairs, I held tight onto my grandad. Not because I thought I might fall, but I was scared for him. He looked as though he was going to go straight from the top to the bottom.

'Are you all right, Grandad? Don't fall.'

He just told me not to be frightened and to hold on tight.

'That's right. You hold onto me son – you'll be all right – don't be frightened.'

40

We both got off the bus, and I watched it drive away. I didn't know where we were, but it was very quiet.

'It's nice here, isn't it Grandad?'

'This is where my dad was born – your greatgrandad.'

It was a lovely place. There weren't many shops and there didn't seem to be many people either. By the bus stop was a big stone thing full of water.

'Hey, Grandad, is that where the horses used to drink?'

'That's right, son. I used to hold my grandad's horse there while it was drinking.'

I couldn't see anything like a basin.

I wondered where it was.

'Where's the basin, Grandad?'

'We've got to walk there. C'mon.'

We went away from the main street, into a side street, past all these little houses. I don't think any cars ever went down this street 'cos there was washing strung out right across the road – all the way down the street. Outside some of the houses were ladies washing down the front step and scraping that yellow stone on the edges. A lot of the houses had curtains over the front door, so that you could leave the door open and the wind didn't blow in. Mind you, it wasn't cold even though it was October. It was nice. The sun was shining – not hot – but just nice. When we got further down the street, I saw that it was a cul-de-sac.

'Hey, Grandad, it's a dead-end. We must've come the wrong way.'

Grandad just smiled.

41

'Do you think I'm that old, that I can't remember the way? Here, look.'

He took my hand and showed me the way. Just before the last house in the road was a tiny snicket. It was so narrow that we had to go through behind each other. I wouldn't have even noticed this snicket if my grandad hadn't shown it to me.

'Go on son, through there.'

It was very dark and all you could see was a little speck of light at the other end, so you can tell how long it was.

'You go first, Grandad.'

'No, after you, son.'

I didn't want to go first.

'No, you'd better go first, Grandad, 'cos you know the way, don't you.'

He laughed and put his hand in his pocket and brought out a few boiled sweets.

'Here you are. These are for the journey. Off we go for the last time.'

I was just going to ask him what he meant, but he carried on talking.

'I mean it'll soon be winter, won't it. Come on.'

And off we went through the dark passage. Grandad told me that when he was a kid they used to call it the Black Hole of Calcutta. Soon we reached the other end and it was quite strange 'cos it was like going through a door into the country. We ended up at the top of some steps – high up above the canal basin, and you could see for miles. I could only see one barge though, in the basin.

We went down the steps. There were a hundred and fifteen steps – I counted them. Grandad was going down slowly so I was at the bottom before him.

'Grandad, there are a hundred and fifteen steps there, I counted them. C'mon let's look at that barge.'

I ran over to have a look at it and Grandad followed me.

'It's like a house isn't it, Grandad?'

'It is a house. Someone lives there. C'mon let's sit here and have our sandwiches.'

And we did.

The sun was very big and round, though it wasn't very hot, and the leaves on the trees were golden, and the reflection in the water made the canal look golden. There was nobody else about, and all the noises that you never noticed usually, suddenly sounded special, different. Like the siren that let the workers know it was dinner-time. I've heard sirens lots of times since then but they never sound so sweet. The same with the train. It must have been miles away 'cos I couldn't see any steam or anything, and you had to listen quite hard, but behind the hum of the country and town sounds mixed together, you could hear this knockety-knock.

When we'd finished our sandwiches we walked along the canal. Grandad showed me how to open the lock-gates, and we were both puffed out afterwards 'cos it was hard work. After a while we walked away from the canal, up a country lane. I don't suppose we were really that far away from home, but we seemed to be miles out in the country, and soon we came to a village. My grandad said we'd catch a bus home from there, but first he wanted to show me something, and he took hold of my hand. I didn't have a clue where he was taking me, but I got a shock when we ended up in the grave-yard. It had gone cold now. I wanted to go home.

'C'mon, Grandad, let's go home now.'

But he didn't seem to be listening properly.

'In a minute son, I just want to show you summat.'

And hand in hand we walked among the gravestones.

'There you are, son, there's my plot. That's where I'll be laid to rest.'

I didn't know what to say.

'When, Grandad?'

'Soon'.

He smiled and looked very happy and he bent down and pulled out a couple of weeds. It was a very neat plot.

'C'mon son, we'd best get going now.'

When I told my mum that night that Grandad was going to die soon, she got very cross and told me not to talk like that.

'He's as fit as a fiddle is your grandad. Don't you talk like that.'

It happened three days later – at dinner-time. It came as a great shock to everybody, except of course to me and Grandad.

Notes on The Holiday

Our determined narrator is seen once again here as desperate to be like his friends. While his mother is not willing to let him go on school camp, he is embarrassed about this in front of his friends, and speaks to a teacher about his predicament. We see the theme of bullying begin in this story, one which recurs later in the book.

What do you think?

The narrator experiences a variety of difficult situations in this story. As you read, consider the many emotions he displays as he reacts to the events that occur.

Questions

1. Why does the narrator use the phrase 'I told you' on the first page of the story? Who is he speaking to?

2. List the many things that are annoying or upsetting the narrator in the first four pages of the story.

3. What sort of person is the narrator's mother? Find evidence in the text to support your answer.

4. What do you learn about the character of Norbert in this story? Find evidence in the text to support your answer.

Further activities

1. Look at the conversation between mother and son beginning '"I've told you – you're not going camping"' to '"I bet if I had a dad"' Write out the dialogue, adding the speaker and a verb to reflect the emotions of the conversation, as well as the correct punctuation. Remember you will need to invent a name for our narrator. The first one is done for you:

'"I've told you – you're not going camping. You're far too young,"' frowned mum.

2. Write the letter from Mr Garnett to the narrator's mother. Remember that she is bringing up her son on her own and has little money. Do you think this has something to do with her unwillingness to let him go on the camp? Think carefully about the reasons he might give to persuade her. How might school help the situation?

The Holiday

It wasn't fair. Tony and Barry were going. In fact, nearly all of them in Standard Three and Four were going – except me. It wasn't fair. Why wouldn't my mum let me go?

'I've told you – you're not going camping. You're far too young.'

Huh! She said that last year.

'You said that last year!'

'You can go next year when you're a bit older.'

She'd said that last year, too.

'You said that last year an' all.'

'Do you want a clout?'

'Well you did, Mum, didn't you?'

'Go and wash your hands for tea.'

'Aw, Mum, everybody else is going to school camp. Why can't I?'

Because you're coming to Bridlington with me and your Auntie Doreen like you do every year.

''Cos you're coming to Bridlington with me and your Auntie Doreen like you do every year!'

I told you. Oh, every year the same thing, my mum, me, and my Auntie Doreen at Mrs Sharkey's boarding house. I suppose we'll have that room next door to the lavatory: a double bed for my mum and my Auntie Doreen, and me on a camp bed behind a screen.

'I suppose we'll have that rotten room again.'

'Don't be cheeky! Mrs Sharkey saves that room for me

every year – last week in July and first week in August. It's the best room in the house, facing the sea like that, and nice and handy for the toilets. You know how important that is for your Auntie Doreen.'

'Aw, Mum, I never get any sleep – the sea splashing on one side and my Auntie Doreen on the …aw!'

My mum gave me a great clout right across my head. She just caught my ear and all.

'Aw, bloomin' heck. What was that for?'

'You know very well. Now stop being so cheeky and go and wash your hands.'

'Well, you've done it now. You've dislocated my jaw – that's it now. I'll report you to that RSPCC thing, and they'll sue you. You've really had it now…ow!'

She clouted me again – right in the same place.

'It's not fair. Tony's mum and dad are letting 'im go to school camp, and Barry's. Why won't you let me go?'

She suddenly bent down and put her face right next to mine, right close. She made me jump. Blimey, that moustache was getting longer. I wish she'd do something about it – it's embarrassing to have a mum with a moustache.

'Now, listen to me my lad. What Tony's mum and dad do, and what Barry's mum and dad do, is their lookout. You will come with me and your Auntie Doreen to Bridlington and enjoy yourself like you do every year!'

Huh! Enjoy myself – that's a laugh for a start. How can you enjoy yourself walking round Bridlington town centre all day looking at shops. You can do that at home.

Or else, it was bingo. 'Key-of-the-door, old-age pension, legs-eleven, clickety-click' an' all that rubbish. You could do that at home as well. And when we did get to the beach, I had to spend all day rubbing that oily sun stuff on me Auntie Doreen's back. It was horrible. Then the rain would come down and it was back to bingo. Honest, what's the point of going on holiday if you do everything that you can do at home? You want to do something different. Now camping, that's different. Tony's dad had bought him a special sleeping bag, just for going camping. Huh! I wish I had a dad.

'I bet if I had a dad, he'd let me go to school camp.'

I thought my mum was going to get her mad up when I said that, but she didn't at all.

'Go and wash your hands for tea, love. Your spam fritters will be ready in a minute.'

Ugh. Bloomin' spam fritters! Not worth washing your hands for!

'Yeh. All right.'

I started to go upstairs. Ooh, I was in a right mess now. I'd told all the other lads I was going. Our names had to be in by tomorrow. We had to give Mr Garnett our pound deposit. Well, I was going to go.

I didn't care what my mum said, I was going to go – somehow!

When I got to the top of the stairs, I kicked a tin waste-paper bin on the landing. It fell right downstairs. It didn't half make a clatter.

'What on earth are you doing?'

49

She would have to hear, wouldn't she?

'Eh. It's all right, Mum. I just tripped over the waste-paper bin. It's all right.'

'Oh, stop playing the goat and come downstairs. Your tea's ready.'

What was she talking about, playing the goat? I couldn't help tripping over a waste-paper bin. Well, I couldn't have helped it if I had tripped over it, an' well, I might have done for all she knew. Well, I wasn't going to wash my hands just for spam fritters. Oh, bet we have macaroni cheese an' all. I went straight downstairs.

'Are your hands clean?'

'Yeh.'

'Here we are then. I've made some macaroni cheese as well.'

'Lovely.'

'C'mon. Eat it up quickly then we'll have a nice bit of telly.'

I didn't say anything else about the school camp that night. I knew it was no good. But I was going to go. I'd told Tony and Barry I was going, I'd told all the lads I was going. Somehow, I'd get my own way. When I got to school next morning, I saw Tony and Barry with Norbert Lightowler over by the Black Hole. That's a tiny snicket, only open at one end, where we shove all the new lads on the first day of term. There's room for about twenty kids. We usually get about a hundred in. It's supposed to be good fun, but the new kids don't enjoy it very much. They get to enjoy it the next year.

'Hello, Tony. Hello, Barry.'

Norbert Lightowler spat out some chewing gum. It just missed me.

'Oh, don't say "hello" to me then, will ya?'

'No. And watch where you're spitting your rotten chewing-gum – or you'll get thumped.'

Barry asked us all if we'd brought our pound deposit for school camp. Tony and Norbert had got theirs, of course. Nobody was stopping them going. I made out I'd forgotten mine.

'Oh heck. I must have left mine on the kitchen table.'

'Oh. I see. Well maybe Garnett'll let you bring it tomorrow.'

I didn't say anything, but Norbert did.

'Oh, no. He said yesterday today's the last day. He said anybody not bringing their deposit today wouldn't be able to go. He did, you know.'

'Aw, shurrup, or I'll do you.'

'I'm only tellin' yer.'

'Well, don't bother.'

Tony asked me if I'd learnt that poem for Miss Taylor. I didn't know what he was talking about.

'What poem?'

Norbert knew of course. He brought a book out of his pocket.

'*Drake's Drum.* Haven't you learnt it?'

Oh crikey! *Drake's Drum.* With all this worry about trying to get to school camp, I'd forgotten all about it. Miss Taylor had told us to learn it for this morning.

'We're supposed to know it this morning, you know.'

'I know, Norbert, I know.'

Honest, Norbert just loved to see you in a mess, I suppose 'cos he's usually in trouble himself.

'*I* know it. I spent all last night learning it. Listen:

"Drake he's in his hammock an' a
     thousand mile away.
Captain, art thou sleeping there below?
Slung a' tween the round shot in
     Nombres Dios bay …".'

I snatched the book out of his hands

'Come 'ere. Let's have a look at it.'

'You'll never learn it in time. Bell'll be going in a minute.'

'You were reading it, anyway.'

'I was not. It took me all last night to learn that.'

Barry laughed at him.

'What all last night to learn three lines?'

'No, clever clogs. I mean the whole poem.'

Just then, the bell started going for assembly.

Norbert snatched his book back.

'C'mon, we'd better get into line. Garnett's on playground duty.'

Norbert went over to where our class was lining up. Barry's in Standard Four, so he went over to their column.

'See you at playtime.'

'Yeh. Tarah.'

While we were lining up, we were all talking. Mr

Garnett just stood there with his hands on his hips, staring at us, waiting for us to stop.

'Thank you.'

Some of us heard his voice and stopped talking. Those that didn't carried on.

'Thank you.'

A few more stopped, and then a few more, till the only voice you could hear was Norbert Lightowler's, and as soon as he realised nobody else was talking, he shut up quick.

'Thank you. If I have to wait for silence as long as that at the end of this morning's break, then we shall spend the whole break this afternoon learning how to file up in silence. Do you understand?'

We all just stood there, hardly daring to breathe.

'Am I talking to myself? Do you understand?'

Everybody mumbled 'Yes, Sir', except Norbert Lightowler. He had to turn round and start talking to me and Tony.

'Huh! If he thinks I'm going to spend my playtime filing up in silence, he's got another think coming.'

'Lightowler!'

Norbert nearly jumped out of his skin.

'Are you talking to those boys behind you?'

'No, Sir. I was just telling 'em summat ...'

'Really?'

'Yes, Sir ... er ... I was just ... er ...telling them that we have to give our pound in today, Sir, for school camp, Sir.'

'I want a hundred lines by tomorrow morning: "I must not talk whilst waiting to go into assembly".'

'Aw, Sir.'

'Two hundred.'

He nearly did it again, but stopped just in time, or he'd've got three hundred.

'Right. When I give the word, I want you to go quietly into assembly. And no talking. Right – wait for it. Walk!'

Everybody walked in not daring to say a word. When we got into the main hall, I asked Tony for the book with *Drake's Drum* in, and during assembly, I tried to snatch a look at the poem but, of course, it was a waste of time. Anyway, I was more worried about my pound deposit for Mr Garnett. After prayers, the headmaster made an announcement about it.

'This concerns only the boys in Standards Three and Four. Today is the final day for handing in your school camp deposits. Those of you not in 3B must see Mr Garnett during morning break. Those of you in 3B will be able to hand in your money when Mr Garnett takes you after Miss Taylor's class. Right, School turn to the right. From the front Dismiss! No talking.'

I had another look at the poem while we were waiting for our turn to go.

'Drake he's in his hammock and a
  thousand mile away,
Captain, art thou sleeping there
  below?'

Well, I knew the first two lines. Tony wasn't too bothered. He probably knew it.

'Don't worry. She can't ask everybody to recite it. Most likely she'll ask one of the girls. Anyway, what are you going to do about Garnett? Do you think he'll let you bring your pound deposit tomorrow?'

'Yeh, sure to.'

If only Tony knew that it'd be just as bad tomorrow. I had to get a pound from somewhere. Then I'd have about four weeks to get my mum to let me go. But I had to get me name down today or I'd ... I'd had it. Miss Taylor was already waiting for us when we got into our classroom.

'Come along children. Settle down.'

Miss Taylor took us for English and Religious Instruction.

'Now today, we're going to deal with some parts of the Old Testament.'

Tony and me looked at each other. She'd got mixed up. Today was English and tomorrow was Religious Instruction.

'Now you've all heard of the Ten Commandments...'

Bloomin' hummer. What a let-off. Tony was grinning at me.

'Do any of you know the first of these Ten Commandments?'

Jennifer Greenwood put her hand up. She was the top of the class every year. Everyone reckoned she was Miss Taylor's favourite.

'Yes, Jennifer.'

Jennifer Greenwood wriggled about a bit in her seat and went red. She's always going red.

'Please, Miss, it's English this morning, Miss; it's Religious Instruction tomorrow, Miss.'

Honest, I could've thumped her. Then Norbert put his hand up.

'Yes, Miss. You told us to learn *Drake's Drum* for this morning, Miss.'

I leaned across to Tony.

'I'll do him at playtime.'

'Quite right, Norbert. Thank you for reminding me. Now, who will recite it for me?'

Everybody shoved their hands up shouting, 'Miss, Miss, me Miss, Miss', so I thought I'd better look as keen as the rest of them.

'Miss! Miss! Miss!'

I stretched my hand up high. I got a bit carried away. I was sure she'd pick one of the girls.

'Me, Miss. Please, Miss. Me, Miss!'

She only went and pointed at me. I couldn't believe it.

'Me, Miss?'

'Yes. You seem very keen for once. Stand up and speak clearly.'

I stood up as slowly as I could. My chair scraped on the floor and made a noise like chalk on the blackboard.

'Hurry up, and lift your chair up. Don't push it like that.'

Everybody was lookin' at me. Norbert who sits in the front row had turned round and was grinning.

'Er … um *Drake's Drum* … by Henry Newbolt…'

Miss Taylor lifted up her finger.

'*Sir* Henry Newbolt!'

'Yes, Miss.'

I was glad she stopped me. Anything to give me more time.

'Carry on.'

I took a deep breath. I could feel Norbert still grinning at me.

'Ahem. *Drake's Drum* … by Sir Henry Newbolt.' I stopped: then I took another deep breath …

'Drake is in his cabin and a thousand mile away…'

I stopped again. I knew after the next line, I'd be in trouble.

'Cap'n, art thou sleeping down below …'

The whole class was listening. I didn't know what I was going to say next. I took another breath and I was just about to tell Miss Taylor I couldn't remember any more, when Norbert burst out laughing. Miss Taylor went over to him.

'What are you laughing at, Norbert?'

'Nothing, Miss.'

'You think you can do better – is that it?'

'No, Miss.'

'Stand up!'

Norbert stood up. Miss Taylor looked at me. 'Well done. That was a very dramatic opening. Sit down, and we'll see if Norbert Lightowler can do as well.'

I couldn't believe it. Tony could hardly keep his face straight.

Norbert went right through the poem. Miss Taylor had to help him once or twice, but he just about got through. Miss Taylor told him he hadn't done badly, but not quite as well as me. After that a few of the others recited it, and then we went on to do some English grammar.

After Miss Taylor, we had Mr Garnett. He gave the girls some arithmetic to do, while he sorted out the deposits for school-camp. He went through the register, and everybody that was going gave him their pound deposit – till he got to me.

'I've forgotten it, Sir.'

'You know today is the last day, don't you ?'

'Yes, Sir.'

'And all the names have to be in this morning? I told you all that yesterday, didn't I?'

'Yes, Sir. Yes, Sir – I'll bring me pound tomorrow, Sir.'

Mr Garnett tapped his pencil.

'I'll put the pound in for you, and I want you to repay me first thing tomorrow morning. All right?'

'Er … um … yes, Sir. I think so, Sir.'

'You do want to go to school camp?'

'Yes, Sir.'

'Right then. Don't forget to give me your pound tomorrow.'

'No, Sir.'

I didn't know what I was going to do now. I reckoned the best thing was to tell Mr Garnett the truth, so when the bell went for playtime, I stayed behind in the classroom, and I told him about my mum wanting me to go to Bridlington with her and my Auntie Doreen. He told me not to worry, and gave me a letter to give to my mum that night. I don't know what it said, but after my mum had read it, she put it in her pocket and said she'd give me a pound for Mr Garnett in the morning.

'Can I go to camp, then?'

'Yes, if that's what you want.'

'I don't mind coming to Bridlington with you and Auntie Doreen, if you'd rather.'

My mum just got hold of my face with both her hands.

'No, love, you go to school camp and enjoy yourself.'

So I did – go to school camp, that is – but I didn't enjoy myself. It was horrible. They put me in a tent with Gordon Barraclough: he's a right bully and he gets everybody on to his side 'cos they're all scared of him. I wanted to go in Tony and Barry's tent, but Mr Garnett said it would upset all his schedules, so I was stuck with Gordon Barraclough and his gang. They made me sleep right next to the opening so when it rained, my sleeping-bag got soaked. And they thought it was dead funny to pull my clothes out of my suitcase (my mum couldn't afford a rucksack) and throw them all over the place.

'Huh! Fancy going camping with a suitcase!'

'Mind your own business, Barraclough! My mum couldn't afford a proper rucksack. Anyway, I'm off to Bridlington on Sunday.'

And I meant it. Sunday was parents visiting day, and my mum and Auntie Doreen were coming to see me on their way to Bridlington. So I was going to pack up all my stuff and go with them. Huh I couldn't stand another week with Gordon Barraclough. I wish I'd never come.

So on Sunday morning after breakfast in the big marquee, I packed everything into my suitcase and waited for my mum and my Auntie Doreen to come. They arrived at quarter to eleven.

'Hello, love. Well, isn't it grand here. You are having a nice time, aren't you?'

'Yeh, it's not bad, but I want to tell you summat.'

My mum wasn't listening. She was looking round the camp-site.

'Well, it's all bigger than I thought. Is this your tent here?'

She poked her 'ead through the flap. I could hear her talking to Gordon Barraclough and the others.

'No! No! No! Don't move boys. Well, haven't you got a lot of room in here? It's quite deceiving from the outside.'

Her head came out again.

'Here, Doreen, you have a look in here. It's ever so roomy.'

She turned back to Gordon Barraclough.

'Well, bye-bye boys. Enjoy the rest of your holiday. And thank you for keeping an eye on my little lad.'

I could hear them all laughing inside the tent. I felt sick.

'Mum, I want to ask you something.'

'In a minute love, in a minute. Let's just see round the camp, and then we'll have a little natter before your Auntie Doreen and me go. Oh, and I want to say hello to Mr Garnett while I'm here. You know, on the way here today, I kept saying wouldn't it be lovely if I could take you on to Bridlington with us. Wasn't I, Doreen? But now I'm here, I can see you're all having a real good time together. You were right, love, it's much better to be with your friends than with two fuddy-duddies like us, eh, Doreen? Well, c'mon love, aren't you going to show us round? We've got to get our bus for Bridlington soon.'

I showed them both round the camp-site, and they went off just before dinner. I didn't feel like anything to eat myself. I just went to the tent and unpacked my suitcase.

Notes on The Gang-hut

'The Gang-hut' describes the normal pleasures and tensions of being part of a group and the battle for power between friends. Its main focus is growing up, as we see first Barry and then Tony reject being part of 'the gang' for varying reasons.

What do you think?
When observing groups of people it is often interesting to watch the dynamics between them. As you read 'The Gang-hut' pay close attention to who holds the power in the relationships and the reasons why each of the characters say what they do. Barry might come across as the strongest character, but do you notice how insecure he is?

Questions
1. Give three reasons why Barry is the initial leader of the gang. Look from 'At last I was in the den' (page 64) to '"Well, first I've got to give you the secret seal – the curse of "The Silent Three".' (page 68) to find evidence in the text to prove your answers.
2. What words would you use to describe Barry's behaviour from the disagreement over the seal to when he wrecks the gang hut?
3. Which sections of the story portray the narrator as rather immature and naive?
4. Look at the last line of the story. How has the narrator changed and why do you think this line is important?

Further activity
What furniture is in the gang-hut in the story? What kind of things would you put in it to make it more cosy if it was your hut?

Imagine you have been given £50 to spend on furnishing the hut. You must buy the following items as cheaply as possible: chest of drawers, sofa or chairs, curtains and one luxury item such as a TV or music system.

Look in the classified ads of your local paper and write down the item, price and phone number of the things you would buy for the hut. You might like to turn this into a competition with your class to see who can furnish the hut for the least amount of money. Give yourself a time limit!

The Gang-hut

We used to have a gang-hut – Barry, Tony, and me. It was smashing. It used to be in Tony's back garden – in fact I think it's still there. I remember one of the last meetings we ever had – it weren't long after August Bank holiday. I went to the gang-hut straight after school. There were a short-cut you could take over a broken wall – you got a bit mucky, but it were quicker. I got to the hut and knocked the secret knock, two quick knocks – a pause – then followed by three more.

'Give the password.'

That was Barry – he was our leader. I stared at the door which had 'The Silent Three' painted on it (I'd done that), and thought.

'What password?'

'What do you mean – what password?'

'What do *you* mean – what do I mean – what password?'

Barry's voice suddenly became deeper, and rather bossy.

'Well, if you'd attended the last gang meeting, you would have known what password!'

Oh, course, that's why I didn't know this blooming password that Barry was talking about. Course, I didn't go to the last gang meeting. How can you go on Bank Holiday Monday? I'd gone with my mum and Auntie Doreen to Scarborough – aye, and it rained all blooming day. I'd felt a bit daft carrying my bucket and spade and ship on the sea front when it was pouring with rain. Yes, and when I'd cheeked my Auntie Doreen off my mum had hit me, and I'd cried – even though it didn't hurt.

'Come on, Barry – tell us what the password is.'

'Well, you haven't to tell anybody.'

'Course not.'

'All right then – it's "Ouvrez la porte".'

'Y'what.'

'"Ouvrez la porte".'

I didn't know what he were talking about.

'It's a blooming long password, isn't it?'

'It's three words – they're French. Not many people will know what it means.'

'What does it mean?'

'It means "open the door".'

'It's a bit ordinary, isn't it?'

'Not if you say it in French.'

'Yes, I suppose so. Anyway, open the door.'

'Say the password!'

'You know it's me – let us in!'

'Say the password!'

'Oh, all right – "Ouvrez la porte".'

At last I was in the den. It was only small – but at least it was ours – Barry's, Tony's and mine – that is – 'The Silent Three' – and now that we'd got a lock and key from Barry's dad, nobody else could get in. Come to think of it, neither could me and Tony, 'cos Barry always kept the key, seeing as his Dad had given us the lock. Tony had said that *he* should keep the key 'cos the den was in his back garden. I'd agreed – not that I wanted Tony to have the key either, but Barry always got things his way – he used to be like that a lot, Barry did, pushing his weight around and telling us how much better he did things than we did. Barry started going on about Tony being late.

'Where's Tony, isn't he coming?'

Tony was in the same class as me.

'Yes, but Miss Taylor kept him in for eating in class. Rotten thing. She's always keeping people in, y'know.'

'Yes, I know. She took us last year.'

Barry was in Standard Four and was going in for his scholarship in December. Tony and me were only in Standard Three. If I'd been taking my scholarship, I'd have been scared stiff, but Barry didn't seem to be.

'Eh, Barry, do you think you'll be scared when you take your scholarship?'

'Yeh, course, everybody gets scared. Wouldn't you?'

'Oh, yeh, I know everybody gets scared, but I just wondered if you did. Which grammar school do you want to go to if you pass?'

'Oh, I don't know – same as my brother I suppose – I don't know.'

Just then, there were two knocks on the door, followed by three more.

'Hey Barry, that might be Tony.'

'What do you mean, might be Tony – it must be Tony – he's the only other one who knows the secret knock, isn't he?'

'Oh, yeh – eh, ask him the password – go on – ask him!'

'I'm going to, don't you worry. Give the password!'

I heard Tony's voice stuttering, trying to think of the password. Oh, ho, he'd forgotten it. He didn't know it. I was right glad he didn't know it.

'Do you know it? Do you know it? You can't come in if you don't know it, can he, Barry?'

'Hang on, I'm thinking. I'll get it, don't tell me. Err … I know! "Our the report".'

'No, "Ouvrez la porte".'

'Well, near enough, wasn't it, let us in.'

'All right, come on.' Barry opened the door and let Tony in.

'Now we all know the password, don't we.'

I knew Barry would say something.

'You should have known it before. I shouldn't really have let you in.'

'Well, I nearly knew it, didn't I, Barry?'

Tony looked at Barry for some kind of praise. Although Tony and me didn't really like Barry being the leader of 'The Silent Three', we accepted him as such, and also accepted his decisions on certain gang matters. It was Barry, for instance, who had decided on the gang's policy, which was 'to rob the rich to help the poor', 'cos that was what Robin Hood did – although it was Tony who had thought of the name 'The Silent Three'.

We had lots of things in the gang-hut. There was a window, with a frame which opened and closed on proper hinges. You had to admire Barry 'cos he'd made that – it was very clever. Of course, there was no real glass in it, but there was some sacking which kept nosy parkers out. There was also a picture on one of the stone walls – it showed a lady, dressed in a long white robe, holding a little baby on her knee – and the baby had long curly hair and it didn't have any clothes on – but you couldn't tell if it was a boy or a girl. Barry didn't like it 'cos he thought it looked soppy. Tony said his grandma had given it to him, and that they ought to be glad they had it 'cos he bet there weren't many gangs that had a picture. I thought it looked nice.

There was also a table, which had two drawers – one for Barry, and one for me and Tony to share. We kept all sorts of things in it – from a rubber stamp which said 'Albert Holdsworth (Worsteds) Limited' to half a potato which, when you dipped it into some paint, and stamped it, said 'The Silent Three'. We had one chair, and we took it in turns to sit in it, and two orange boxes. Also, there was a small carpet which my mum was going to throw away. She'd said to me – 'Oh, you don't want that dirty old thing'. And I'd said yes, I did – and I'd muttered something about the fight against evil and 'The Curse of the Silent Three', but by then my mum wasn't listening. Anyway the most important thing was that I'd got the carpet and proudly presented it to Barry and Tony at the next gang meeting, and what had really pleased me was that the other two were impressed as I'd hoped they'd be. Well, that was really all we had in the gang-hut, oh, except two candles which were kept for emergency.

'What shall we do then?'

Tony looked at Barry for an answer. This was usually the way gang meetings started, and most times the question was directed towards Barry, 'cos his were usually the best ideas, and anyway, we always did what he suggested.

'Well, first I've got to give you the secret seal – the curse of "The Silent Three".'

I knew this was what Barry would say, and it was just what I didn't want.

'Oh, not again, Barry. I got into trouble with my mum last time. It took ages to get it off. My mum says I haven't to let you do it again.'

This didn't bother Barry.

'You've got to have the Secret Seal or else you're not a member of "The Silent Three" – isn't that right, Tony?'

Tony had to agree, although I knew by his face, *he* wasn't that keen to have the stamp *either*.

'Anyway, it won't go on so strong this time, 'cos I won't put any more paint on.'

Barry took out the half potato from his drawer. It had dried blue paint on it from the last time we'd used it, and he spat on it to make it wet.

'Ooh, we'll all get diseases!'

'No, you won't. Hold out your hand.'

'No, I'm not having your spit all over me.'

'C'mon, you've got to have it or you'll be banned from "The Silent Three". You've got to have it, hasn't he, Tony?'

Tony nodded in agreement, but he was even more

reluctant now than he was earlier on. Barry looked right at me.

'C'mon – are you going to have it or not?'

I just sat there.

'Well, you should have let us do our own spitting.'

'Well, it's too late now. Are you going to have it or not?'

'No, I'm not!'

Barry just lost his temper then and threw the potato on the floor.

'Well, I'm not bothered about the secret seal anyway – or the gang-hut for that matter. I was only joining in to please you kids!'

Tony and me, he meant. I was really shocked – 'cos I mean after all he was the leader of 'The Silent Three'. I didn't know what to say. I just sat there.

Tony picked up the potato, I held my hand out and he stamped it – then he stamped his own. He tried to stamp Barry's hand, but Barry wouldn't let him. 'The Silent Three' sat in silence – me and Tony waiting for the secret seal to dry and Barry – well – just not interested.

When the secret seal had dried, I started to talk to Barry.

'Eh, Barry, you know that kid in your class with that big red patch on his face …'

'That's a birthmark!'

'Yer, that big red birthmark. He was crying his head off in the lavatory this morning.'

'Yeh, I know, his grandad died last night. He went home at dinner time.'

'I remember my grandad. We used to go for walks when

I was little. He's dead now. I don't remember my grandma though. She died when I was two.'

'What about your other grandad and grandma?' I didn't know what Barry was talking about. I looked at him.

'What other grandad and grandma?'

'Your other grandad and grandma. You know your other grandad and grandma. You have two grandads and grandmas, you know. Oh, don't you even know that?'

Tony said that he had two an' all.

'Yes, I've got two grandads and grandmas. I've got my grandad and my grandma Atkinson, and my grandad and my grandma Spencer.'

Barry seemed to be really enjoying this.

'Oh, don't you know you have two grandads and grandmas?'

'All I know is, I've never seen my grandma, 'cos she died when I was two, and my grandad's dead an all.'

And as far as I was concerned, that was that, although really it surprised me to hear that Barry and Tony both had two sets of grandads and grandmas. Why hadn't I – I'd have to ask my mum.

Tony and Barry started talking about swimming.

'We start swimming lessons next year. Tony meant me and him. You didn't have swimming lessons until you got into Standard Four. Barry had been having lessons for a while – he was quite good.

'I can do two lengths, and a half a length on my back.'

70

Tony could float a bit.

'I'm right looking forward to having swimming lessons, aren't you?'

I wasn't really looking forward to having swimming lessons. To be quite honest, I was scared stiff.

'Yes, I suppose so. I might be a bit scared though.'

'What for?' Oh, it was all right for Barry to talk.

'What is there to be scared about. You scared you might drown?'

Yes, I was.

'Course I'm not.'

I'd only been to the swimming baths once in my life, and somebody had pushed me in then. It was very scaring – I thought I was going to drown that time. The pool attendant had pulled me out and thumped the lad who'd pushed me in. I'd never been to the baths again since then. Barry was still going on about being scared.

'There's nowt to be scared of, y'know. It's dead easy, swimming is. Isn't it, Tony?'

'I don't know, I can't swim. I can float a bit.'

'Ah, floating's easy – anyone can float.'

Huh, I couldn't! I was fed up with this talk about swimming. It reminded me too much of what was to come. So I started to talk about something else.

'Eh, it'll be bonfire night soon.'

This got us all quite excited and Barry said we'd have the biggest bonfire in the neighbourhood. Tony said we should start collecting wood 'cos it was the end of August already.

'We'll have to go down the woods – we could go down on Sunday afternoon.'

Barry agreed, but I said I'd have to ask my mum. 'You're always having to ask her. Can't you do anything without asking her?'

'Course I can, but she doesn't like me going down those woods.'

I had to go then 'cos my mum told me I had to be in by a quarter to six. Tony had to go too, 'cos he was sleeping at our house that weekend, 'cos his mum was going away to stay with his big sister for a few days, who was married and lived in Manchester.

'My mum says by the time she gets back from Manchester, I'll be an uncle.'

So the gang meeting ended. Tony and me had to go to town next day with my mum, but we said we'd see Barry at the gang-hut at about four o'clock. Barry said all right, and that he was going home to see if he could find any empty bottles to take back to the shop so he'd have some money to buy toffees for the Saturday morning matinee.

Barry started locking up the hut.

'Eh, are you two going to the pictures tomorrow morning?'

'I don't know. We might do. See you tomorrow afternoon anyway. Tarah.'

I asked my mum that night why I didn't have two grandads and grandmas like Tony and Barry, but she just told me not to ask silly questions and to get on with my supper.

We didn't go to the matinee next day 'cos my mum said that we both had to have our hair cut before going into town that afternoon. I tried to get out of it, but I couldn't, and Tony didn't help either 'cos he agreed with my mum and said we did really need our hair cut.

Anyway that was what happened, and at about quarter to four, we came back from town with lots of shopping. Tony and me changed out of our best suits – mine was brand new – I only got it just before t'Bank Holiday – and we went straight over to the gang-hut. Well, we just got over the broken wall into Tony's backyard, and I knew something was wrong – and when I realised what it was I just couldn't believe it; the whole gang-hut was wrecked. Honest, I'll never forget it. The door was wide open and inside the place was in a real mess – the two orange boxes were broken, the table was knocked over, the picture (of the lady) was lying on the floor. The window frame was pulled away from the hinges.

It was awful. All I could feel was this great thumping in my head.

'Hey, Tony, I wonder who did it?'

'Barry did. Look!'

He pointed to the door, and instead of 'The Silent Three', it said 'The Silent Two'.

'Why did he do it?'

Tony shrugged his shoulders and said he'd probably felt like it.

Neither of us knew then why Barry had done it, but Tony somehow didn't seem too bothered neither. I suppose he knew that he'd be the leader of the gang now. *I* just couldn't understand it at all – why would Barry wreck the whole gang-hut like this, especially since he had built most of it himself – specially the window frame.

When Tony left the gang, I became leader – for a while – Tony didn't do anything like wrecking the hut, nor did I when I left – we just got tired of it and – well … lost interest.

Some other younger lads used the hut for their meetings after us, but Barry, Tony and me weren't bothered. We didn't care who had the gang-hut now.

Notes on The Fib

At the centre of this story is the line 'That's why the fib became a lie'. In the first two stories of the book we were encouraged to consider the nature of stealing and, in this story, once again, *A Northern Childhood* makes us think about moral issues: is there a difference between a fib and a lie?

What do you think?

As you read through the story, think about the things the narrator does that are blameful. Do you think he lies just to make life easier for himself? While that's a common reason for lying, is it a good enough one? Do you think that this story encourages young people to lie?

Questions

1. Explain what the narrator means when he says 'That's why the fib became a lie.'
2. Which do you think is the most exciting paragraph in this story for the reader? Give reasons for your choice.
3. What does the story add to what we have learnt about Norbert Lightowler in 'The Holiday'.
4. George Layton often ends these stories with an unexpected twist in events. Compare and contrast the ending of 'The Fib' with those of 'The Holiday' and 'The Balaclava Story'.

Further activity

The combination of the topics of sport and violence in this chapter are an interesting reflection of the language we find in newspaper sports articles.

- Re-read the section beginning 'Norbert just laughed, and Gordon thumped him' to '"He could've choked me"'. Underline any verbs that are effective in conveying the aggression of the fight.
- Underline any words in this section that are to do with animal behaviour.
- Look through the sports section of a newspaper. Pick out three quotations that use the language of war, violence or animal-like behaviour to describe a football match.

The Fib

Ooh, I wasn't half snug and warm in bed, I could near my mum calling me to get up, but it was ever so cold. Every time I breathed, I could see a puff of air. The window was covered with frost. I just couldn't get myself out of bed.

'Are you up? I've called you three times already.'

'Yes, Mum, 'course I am.'

I knew it was a lie, but I just wanted to have a few more minutes in bed. It was so cosy.

'You'd better be, because I'm not telling you again.'

That was another lie. She was always telling me again.

'Just you be quick, young man, and frame yourself, or you'll be late for school.'

Ooh school! If only I didn't have to go. Thank goodness we were breaking up soon for Christmas. I don't mind school – I quite like it sometimes. But today was Monday, and Mondays was football, and I hate blooming football. It wouldn't be so bad if I had proper kit, but I had to play in these old-fashioned shorts and boots that my mum had got from my Uncle Kevin. They were huge. Miles too big for me. Gordon Barraclough's mum and dad had bought him a Bobby Charlton strip and Bobby Charlton boots. No wonder he's a better player than me. My mum said she couldn't see what was wrong with my kit. She couldn't understand that I felt silly, and all the other lads laughed at me – even Tony, and he's my best friend. She just said she wasn't going to waste good money on new boots and shorts, when I had a perfectly good set already.

'But Mum, they all laugh at me – especially Gordon Barraclough.'

'Well laugh back at them. You're big enough aren't you? Don't be such a jessie.'

She just couldn't understand.

'You tell them your Uncle Kevin played in those boots when he was a lad, and he scored thousands of goals.'

Blimey, that shows you how old my kit is!

My Uncle Kevin's 29! I snuggled down the bed a bit more, and pulled the pillow under the blankets with me.

'I'm coming upstairs and if I find you not up, there'll be trouble. I'm not telling you again.'

Oh 'eck! I forced myself out of bed on to the freezing lino and got into my underpants. Ooh, they were cold! Blooming daft this. Getting dressed, going to school, and getting undressed again to play rotten football. I looked out of the window and it didn't half look miserable. I *felt* miserable. I *was* miserable. Another 90 minutes standing between the posts, letting in goal after goal, with Gordon Barraclough shouting at me:

'Why didn't you dive for it, you lazy beggar?'

Why didn't *he* dive for it? Why didn't *he* go in goal? Why didn't he shut his rotten mouth? Oh no, *he* was always centre forward wasn't he, 'cos *he* was Bobby Charlton.

As I stood looking out of the window, I started wondering how I could get out of going to football

I know, I'd tell my mum I wasn't feeling well. I'd tell her I'd got a cold. No, a sore throat. No, she'd look. Swollen glands. Yes, that's what I'd tell her, swollen glands. No, she'd feel. What could I say was wrong with me? Earache, yes, earache, and I'd ask her to write me a note. I'd ask her after breakfast. Well, it was only a fib wasn't it?

'You're very quiet. Didn't you enjoy your breakfast?'

'Err … well … I don't feel very well, Mum. I think I've got earache.'

'You *think* you've got earache?'

'I mean I *have* got earache – definitely – in my ear.'

'Which ear?'

'What?'

'You going deaf as well? I said, which ear?'

'Err … my right ear. Perhaps you'd better write me a note to get me off football …'

'No, love, it'll be good for you to go to football, get some fresh air. I'll write to Mr Melrose and ask him to let you go in goal, so you don't have to run around too much.'

She'd write a note to *ask* if I could go in …!

Melrose didn't need a note for me to go in goal. I was *always* shoved in goal. Me and Norbert Lightowler were always in goal, 'cos we were the worst players.

Norbert didn't care. He was never bothered when people shouted at him. He just told them to get lost. He never even changed for football. He just stuffed his trousers into his socks and said it was a track suit. He nearly looked as daft as me in my Uncle Kevin's old kit.

'Mum, don't bother writing me a note. I'll be all right.'

'I'm only thinking of you. If you've got earache I don't want you to run around too much. I don't want you in bed for Christmas.'

'I'll be OK.'

Do you know, I don't think my mum believed I'd got earache. I know I was fibbing, but even if I had got earache, I don't think she'd have believed me. Mums are like that.

'Are you sure you're all right?'

'Yes, I'll be O.K.'

How could my mum know that when I was in goal I ran around twice as much, anyway? Every time the other team scored, I had to belt halfway across the playing field to fetch the ball back.

'Well, finish your Rice Krispies. Tony'll be here in a minute.'

Tony called for me every morning. I was never ready. I was just finishing my toast when I heard my mum let him in. He came through to the kitchen.

'Aw, come on. You're never ready.'

'I won't be a minute.'

'We'll be late, we'll miss the football bus.'

We didn't have any playing fields at our school, so we had a special bus to Bankfield Top, about two miles away.

'If we miss the bus I'll do you.'

'We won't miss the bus. Stop panicking …'

I wouldn't have minded missing it.

'…anyway we might not have football today. It's very frosty.'

'Course we will. Y'aren't half soft, you.'

It was all right for Tony, he wasn't bad at football. Nobody shouted at him.

'It's all right for you. Nobody shouts at you.'

'Well, who shouts at you?'

'Gordon Barraclough.'

'You don't want to take any notice. Now hurry up.'

My mum came in with my kit.

'Yes, hurry up or you'll miss your bus for football.'

'We won't miss our rotten bus for rotten football.'

She gave me a clout on the back of my head. Tony laughed.

'And you can stop laughing, Tony Wainwright,' and she gave him a clout, as well. 'Now go on, both of you.'

We ran to school and got there in plenty of time. I knew we would.

Everybody was getting on the bus. We didn't have to go to assembly when it was football. Gordon Barraclough was on the top deck with his head out of the window. He saw me coming.

'Hey, Gordon Banks ...'

He always called me that, 'cos he thinks Gordon Banks was the best goalie ever. He reckons he was called Gordon after Gordon Banks.

'Hey, Gordon Banks – how many goals are you going to let in today?'

Tony nudged me.

'Don't take any notice.'

'Come on, Gordon Banks, how many goals am I going to get against you …?'

Tony nudged me again.

'Ignore him.'

'…or am I going to be lumbered with you on my side, eh?'

'He's only egging you on. Ignore him.'

Yes, I'll ignore him. That's the best thing. I'll ignore him.

'If you're on my side, Gordon Banks, you'd better not let any goals in, or I'll do you.'

Just ignore him, that's the best thing.

'Get lost Barraclough, you rotten big-head.'

I couldn't ignore him. Tony was shaking his head.

'I told you to ignore him.'

'I couldn't.'

Gordon still had his head out of the window.

'I'm coming down to get you.'

And he would've done, too, if it hadn't been for Norbert. Just as Gordon was going back into the bus, Norbert wound the window up, so Gordon's head was stuck. It must've hurt him – well, it could have choked him.

'You're a maniac, Lightowler. You could have choked me.'

Norbert just laughed, and Gordon thumped him, right in the neck, and they started fighting. Tony and me ran up the stairs to watch. They were rolling in the aisle. Norbert got on top of Gordon and put his knees on his shoulders. Everybody was watching now, and shouting:

'Fight! Fight! Fight! Fight!'

The bell hadn't gone for assembly yet, and other lads from the playground came out to watch.

'Fight! Fight! Fight! Fight!'

Gordon pushed Norbert off him, and they rolled under a seat. Then they rolled out into the aisle again, only this time Gordon was on top. He thumped Norbert right in the middle of his chest. Hard. It hurt him, and Norbert got his mad up. I really wanted him to do Gordon.

'Go on Norbert, do him.'

Just then, somebody clouted me on the back of my head, right where my mum had hit me that morning. I turned round to belt whoever it was.

'Who do you think you're thumping …? Oh, morning, Mr Melrose.'

He pushed me away, and went over to where Norbert and Gordon were still fighting. He grabbed them both by their jackets, and pulled them apart. He used to be in the Commandos did Mr Melrose.

'Animals! You're a pair of animals! What are you?'

Neither of them said anything. He was still holding them by their jackets. He shook them.

'What are you? Lightowler?'

'A pair of animals.'

'Gordon?'

'A pair of animals, sir. It wasn't my fault, sir. He started it, sir. He wound up that window, sir and I got my head stuck. He could have choked me, sir.'

Ooh, he was a right tell-tale was Barraclough.

'Why was your head out of the window in the first place?'

'I was just telling someone to hurry up, sir.'

He's a liar as well, but he knew he was all right with Melrose, 'cos he's his favourite.

'And then Lightowler wound up the window, for no reason, sir. He could've choked me.'

Melrose didn't say anything. He just looked at Norbert. Norbert looked back at him with a sort of smile on his face. I don't think he meant to be smiling. It was because he was nervous.

'I'm sick of you, Lightowler, do you know that? I'm sick and tired of you. You're nothing but a trouble-maker.'

Norbert didn't say anything. His face just twitched a bit. It was dead quiet on the bus. The bell went for assembly and we could hear the other classes filing into school.

'A trouble-maker and a hooligan. You're a disgrace to the school, do you know that Lightowler?'

'Yes sir.'

'I can't wait for the day you leave, Lightowler.'

'Neither can I, sir.'

Melrose's hand moved so fast that it made *everybody* jump – not just Norbert. It caught him right on the side of his face. His face started going red straight away. Poor old Norbert. I didn't half feel sorry for him. It wasn't fair. He was helping me.

'Sir, can I …?'

'Shut up!'

Melrose didn't even turn round, and I didn't need

telling twice. I shut up. Norbert's cheek was getting redder. He didn't rub it though, and it must've been stinging like anything. He's tough is Norbert.

'You're a lout, Lightowler. What are you?'

'A lout, sir.'

'You haven't even got the decency to wear a school blazer.'

Norbert was wearing a grey jacket that was miles too big for him. He didn't have a school blazer.

'Aren't you proud of the school blazer?'

'I suppose so.'

'Why don't you wear one, then?'

Norbert rubbed his cheek for the first time.

'I haven't got a school blazer, sir.'

He looked as though he was going to cry.

'My mum can't afford one.'

Nobody moved. Melrose stared at Norbert.

It seemed ages before he spoke.

'Get out of my sight, Lightowler. Wait in the classroom until we come back from football. And get your hands out of your pockets. The rest of you sit down and be quiet.'

Melrose went downstairs and told the driver to set off. Tony and me sat on the back seat. As we turned right into Horton Road, I could see Norbert climbing on the school wall, and walking along it like a tightrope walker. Melrose must've seen him as well. He really asks for trouble does Norbert.

It's about a ten-minute bus-ride to Bankfield Top. You go into town, through the City Centre and up Bankfield

Road. When we went past the Town Hall, everybody leaned over to look at the Lord Mayor's Christmas tree.

'Back in your seats. You've all seen a Christmas tree before.'

Honestly, Melrose was such a spoil-sport. Course we'd all seen a Christmas tree before – but not as big as that. It must have been about thirty foot tall. There were tons of lights on it as well, *and* there were lights and decorations all round the square and in the shops. Tony said they were being switched on at half-past four that afternoon. He'd read it in the paper. So had know-it-all Gordon Barraclough.

'Yeah, I read that, too. They're being switched on by a mystery celebrity.'

Ooh, a mystery celebrity. Who was it going to be?

'A mystery celebrity? Do you know who it is?'

Gordon looked at me as though I'd asked him what two and two came to.

'Course I don't know who it is. Nobody knows who it is, otherwise it wouldn't be a mystery would it?'

He was right there.

'Well somebody must know who it is, 'cos somebody must've asked him in the first place, mustn't they?'

Gordon gave me another of his looks.

'The Lord Mayor knows. Course he knows, but if *you* want to find out, you have to go and watch the lights being switched on, don't you?'

Tony said he fancied doing that. I did as well, as long as I wasn't too late home for my mum.

'Yeah, it'll be good, but I'll have to be home by half-past five, before my mum gets back from work.'

When we got to Bankfield Top, Melrose told us we had three minutes to get changed. Everybody ran to the temporary changing-room. It's always been called the 'temporary changing-room' ever since anyone can remember. We're supposed to be getting a proper place sometime with hot and cold showers and things, but I don't reckon we ever will.

The temporary changing-room's just a shed. It's got one shower that just runs cold water, but even that doesn't work properly. I started getting into my football togs. I tried to make the shorts as short as I could by turning the waist-band over a few times, but they still came down to my knees. And the boots were great big heavy things. Not like Gordon Barraclough's Bobby Charlton ones. I could've worn mine on either foot – it wouldn't have made any difference.

Gordon was changed first, and started jumping up and down and doing all sorts of exercises. He even had a Manchester United track suit top on.

'Come on Gordon Banks, get out on to the park.'

Get out on to the park! Just 'cos his dad took him over to see Manchester United every other Saturday, he thought he knew it all.

The next hour and a half was the same as usual – rotten. Gordon and Curly Emmott picked sides – as usual. I went in goal – as usual. I nearly froze to death – as usual, and I let in fifteen goals – as usual. Most of the time all you could hear was Melrose shouting: 'Well done, Gordon', 'Go round him, Gordon', 'Good deception, Gordon', 'Give it to Gordon', 'Shoot, Gordon', 'Hard luck, Gordon'.

Ugh! Mind you, he did play well, did Gordon. He's the best player in our year. At least, today, I wasn't on his side so I didn't have him shouting at me all the time – just scoring against me! I thought Melrose was never going to blow the final whistle. When he did, we all trudged back to the temporary changing-room. Even on the way back Gordon was jumping up and down and doing all sorts of funny exercises. He was only showing off to Melrose.

'That's it Gordon, keep warm. Keep the muscles supple. Well played, lad! We'll see you get a trial for United yet.'

Back in the changing-room, Gordon started going on about my football kit. He egged everybody else on.

'Listen Barraclough, this strip belonged to my uncle, and he scored thousands of goals.'

Gordon just laughed.

'Your uncle? Your auntie more like. You look like a big girl.'

'Listen Barraclough, you don't know who my uncle is.'

I was sick of Gordon Barraclough. I was sick of his bullying and his shouting, and his crawling round Melrose. And I was sick of him being a good footballer.

'My uncle is Bobby Charlton!'

That was the fib.

For a split second I think Gordon believed me, then he burst out laughing. So did everyone else. Even Tony laughed.

'Bobby Charlton – your uncle? You don't expect us to believe that do you?'

'Believe what you like – it's the truth.'

Course they didn't believe me. That's why the fib became a lie.

'Cross my heart and hope to die.'

I spat on my left hand. They all went quiet. Gordon put his face close to mine.

'You're a liar.'

I was.

'I'm not. Cross my heart and hope to die.'

I spat on my hand again. If I'd dropped dead on the spot, I wouldn't have been surprised. Thank goodness Melrose came in, and made us hurry on to the bus.

Gordon and me didn't talk to each other much for the rest of the day. All afternoon I could see him looking at me. He was so sure I was a liar, but he just couldn't be certain.

Why had I been so daft as to tell such a stupid lie? Well, it was only a fib really, and at least it shut Gordon Barraclough up for an afternoon.

After school, Tony and me went into town to watch the lights being switched on. Norbert tagged along as well. He'd forgotten all about his trouble with Melrose that morning. He's like that, Norbert. Me, I'd've been upset for days.

There was a crowd at the bottom of the Town Hall steps, and we managed to get right to the front. Gordon was there already. Norbert was ready for another fight, but we stopped him. When the Lord Mayor came out we all clapped. He had his chain on, and he made a speech about the Christmas appeal.

Then it came to switching on the lights.

'…and as you know, ladies and gentlemen, boys and girls, we always try to get someone special to switch on our Chamber of Commerce Christmas lights, and this year is no exception. Let's give a warm welcome to Mr Bobby Charlton …'

I couldn't believe it. I nearly fainted. I couldn't move for a few minutes. Everybody was asking for his autograph. When it was Gordon's turn, I saw him pointing at me. I could feel myself going red. Then, I saw him waving me over. Not Gordon, Bobby Charlton!

I went. Tony and Norbert followed. Gordon was grinning at me.

'You've had it now. You're for it now. I told him you said he's your uncle.'

I looked up at Bobby Charlton. He looked down at me. I could feel my face going even redder. Then suddenly, he winked at me and smiled.

'Hello, son. Aren't you going to say hello to your Uncle Bobby, then?'

I couldn't believe it. Neither could Tony or Norbert. Or Gordon.

'Er … hello … Uncle …er … Bobby.'

He ruffled my hair.

'How's your mam?'

'All right.'

He looked at Tony, Norbert and Gordon.

'Are these your mates?'

'These two are.'

I pointed out Tony and Norbert.

'Well, why don't you bring them in for a cup of tea?'

I didn't understand.

'In where?'

'Into the Lord Mayor's Parlour. For tea. Don't you want to come?'

'Yeah, that'd be lovely ... Uncle Bobby.'

Uncle Bobby! I nearly believed it myself! And I'll never forget the look on Gordon Barraclough's face as Bobby Charlton led Tony, Norbert and me into the Town Hall.

It was ever so posh in the Lord Mayor's Parlour. We had sandwiches without crusts, malt loaf and butterfly cakes. It was smashing. So was Bobby Charlton. I just couldn't believe we were there. Suddenly, Tony kept trying to tell me something, but I didn't want to listen to him. I wanted to listen to Bobby.

'Shurrup, I'm trying to listen to my Uncle Bobby.'

'But do you know what time it is? Six o'clock!'

'Six o'clock! Blimey! I've got to get going. My mum'll kill me.'

I said goodbye to Bobby Charlton.

'Tarah, Uncle Bobby. I've got to go now. Thanks...'

He looked at me and smiled.

'Tarah, son. See you again some time.'

When we got outside, Tony and Norbert said it was the best tea they'd ever had.

I ran home as fast as I could. My mum was already in, of course. I was hoping she wouldn't be too worried. Still, I knew everything would be all right once I'd told her I was late because I'd been having tea in the Lord Mayor's Parlour with Bobby Charlton.

'Where've you been? It's gone quarter past six. I've been worried sick.'

'It's all right, Mum. I've been having tea in the Lord Mayor's Parlour with Bobby Charlton ...'

She gave me such a clout, I thought my head was going to fall off. My mum never believes me – even when I'm telling the truth!

Notes on The Firework Display

The different opinions of the narrator and his mother again cause tension in this story, as the boys compete with the fireworks they are able to buy for bonfire night. The story opens with lively camaraderie between the boys as they collect wood for a big bonfire and in his desire to be respected by his friends, the narrator makes some foolish decisions.

What do you think?
As you read through this story, compare its structure with 'The Holiday'. In the earlier story:
- the narrator wants something
- he does something to get it
- his actions eventually have disappointing consequences.

How do you expect this story to end, in happiness or disaster?

Questions
1. How does the first line of the story capture the reader's attention?
2. How does George Layton add humour to the story through action and dialogue in the first three pages of the story?
3. Why do you think his mother will not allow him to buy fireworks?
4. What do you notice about the narrator in this story that fits in with what you have already learnt about him in previous stories?
5. Comment on the title George Layton chose for this story.

Further activity
Write an article for a local newspaper about the fireworks accident at the house. Think carefully about layout, remembering columns, headlines and pictures. You might want to use a desktop publishing program to help you with this.

Remember a newspaper article needs the five Ws: who, what, when, where, why. You might like to include some of the following:
- brief comments from those involved
- the background to the incident
- witnesses' statements
- general advice about fireworks for the public.

The Firework Display

Norbert was hanging from this branch, swinging his legs about, and trying to break it off. If the Park Ranger came by and saw him, we'd have all been in trouble. Barry got hold of him round the ankles.

'Norbert, I'll do you if you don't come down.'

Norbert pulled his legs free, and moved along the branch towards the trunk. Barry chased after him and tried to pull him down again, but Norbert had managed to hoist himself up on to his tummy and was kicking Barry away.

'Gerroff!'

Barry punched him on the back of his leg.

'Well, get down then, or you'll get us all into trouble. Park Ranger said we could only take dead stuff.'

We were collecting for Bonfire Night. We were going to have the biggest bonfire in the district. It was already about twelve foot high, and it was only Saturday, so there were still two days to go. Three if you counted Monday itself.

We'd built the fire in Belgrave Street where the Council were knocking all the houses down. There was tons of waste ground, so there was no danger, and we'd found two old sofas and three armchairs to throw on the fire.

Norbert dropped from the branch and landed in some dog dirt. Barry and me laughed 'cos he got it on his hands. I told him it served him right for trying to break the branch.

'You're stupid, Norbert. You know the Park Ranger said we could only take the dead branches.'

Norbert was wiping his hands on the grass.

'I thought it *was* dead.'

I threw a stick at him.

'How could it be dead if it's still growing? You're crackers you are, Norbert.'

The stick caught him on his shoulder. It was only a twig.

'Don't you throw lumps of wood at me! How would you like it if I threw lumps of wood at you?'

'Don't be so soft Norbert, it was only a twig.'

Norbert picked up a big piece of wood, and chucked it at me. Luckily it missed by miles.

'You're mad, Norbert. You want to be put away. You're a blooming maniac.'

'You started it. You shouldn't have chucked that stick at me.'

He went back to wiping his hands on the grass.

'Was it heckers like a stick. It was a little twig, and it's no good wiping your hands on the grass, you'll never get rid of that pong.'

Suddenly, Norbert ran at me, waving his hands towards my face. I got away as fast as I could but he kept following.

'If you touch me with those smelly hands … I'm warning you Norbert.'

I picked up a brick, and threatened him with it.

'I'm telling you Norbert …'

Just then I heard a voice from behind me.

'Hey!'

It was the Park Ranger.

'You lads, stop acting the goat. You!'

He meant me.

'What do you think you're doing with that?'

'Nowt …'

I dropped the brick on the ground.

'…Just playing.'

'That's how accidents are caused. Now come on lads, you've got your bonfire wood. On your way now.'

I gave Norbert another look, just to let him know that I'd meant it. He sniffed his hands.

'They don't smell, anyway.'

Barry and me got hold of the bottom branches and started dragging the pile, and Barry told Norbert to follow on behind.

'Norbert, you pick up anything that falls off, and chuck it back on. Come on, Tony and Trevor'll be wondering where we are.'

Trevor Hutchinson and Tony were back at Belgrave Street guarding the fire. You had to do that to stop other lads from nicking all the wood you've collected, or from setting fire to it. Not that it mattered, 'cos if they did we'd just nick somebody else's.

Mind you, I wouldn't have been bothered if our fire *had* gone up in smoke, 'cos it didn't look like my mum was going to let me go on Monday anyway. And even if she did, she certainly wouldn't let me have my own fireworks. I'd been on at her all morning about it while she'd been ironing.

'But why, Mum? All the other lads at school are having their own fireworks, all of 'em. Why can't I?'

Why was my mum so difficult? Why did she have to be so old fashioned?

'Go on, Mum …'

She just carried on with her ironing.

'It washes well this shirt.'

It was that navy blue one my Auntie Doreen had given me for my birthday last February.

'I'd like to get you another one. I must ask your Auntie Doreen where she bought it.'

'Why can't I have my own fireworks, Mum? Why?' She just wouldn't listen.

'I'm old enough aren't I?'

'Will you remind me there's a button missing off this shirt?'

'Aren't I?'

'I don't know what you do with the buttons off your shirts. You must eat them.'

She was driving me mad.

'Mum, are you going to let me have my own fireworks this year or not?'

She slammed the iron down.

'Oh, stop mithering will you? You're driving me mad.'

'Well are you or aren't you?'

She put the shirt on a pile, and pulled a sheet out of the washing basket.

'No! You'll come with me and your Auntie Doreen to the firework display at the Children's Hospital like you do every year, and if you don't stop mithering you won't even be doing that. Now give me a hand with this.'

She gave me one end of the sheet and we shook it.

'It's not fair. Tony's having his own fireworks this year, and he's three weeks younger than me, and Trevor Hutchinson's mum and dad have got him a £5 box.'

We folded the sheet twice to make it easier to iron. 'Then they've got more money than sense, that's all I can say.

'I'll pay you back out of my spending money, honest.'

My mum gave me one of her looks.

'Oh yes? Like you did with your bike? One week you kept that up. I'm still waiting for the rest.'

That wasn't fair, it was ages ago.

'That's not fair, that was ages ago.'

I'd promised my mum that if she bought me a new bike – a drop handle-bar – I'd pay her some back every week out of my spending money. But she didn't give me enough. How could I pay her back?

'You don't give me enough spending money. I don't have enough to pay you back.'

'Why don't you save some? You don't have to spend it all do you?'

Bloomin' hummer! What's the point of calling it spending money, if you don't spend it?

'Mum, it's called *spending* money, isn't it? That means it's for *spending*. If it was meant for saving, people would call it *saving* money. You're only trying to get out of it.'

I was fed up. My mum was only trying to get out of getting me fireworks. She came over.

'Don't you be so cheeky young man. Who do you think you're talking to?'

I thought for a minute she was going to clout me one.

'Well… even if I had some money saved, you wouldn't let me buy fireworks, would you?'

She didn't say anything.

'Well would you … Eh?'

She told me not to say 'Eh' 'cos it's rude. I don't think it's rude. It's just a word.

'Well, would you, Mum? If I had my own money, I bet you wouldn't let me buy fireworks with it.'

'Stop going on about it, for goodness sake. You're not having any fireworks and that's final.'

It blooming well wasn't final. I wanted my own fireworks this year and *that* was final. Blimey, kids much younger than me have their own fireworks. Why shouldn't I?

'Apart from being a waste of money they're dangerous.'

Dangerous. Honest, she's so old-fashioned, my mum.

'Mum, there are instructions on every firework. As long as you light the blue touch paper and retire, they're not dangerous.'

She started going on about how many people were taken to hospital every Bonfire Night, and how many children were injured, and how many limbs were lost, and if all fireworks were under supervised care like they are at the Children's Hospital, then there'd be far less accidents. She went on and on. I'd heard it all before.

'But I'll be careful Mum, I promise. Please let me have my own fireworks.'

That's when she clouted me.

'Are you going deaf or summat?'

'What?'

It was Norbert shouting from behind.

'Y'what Norbert?'

He picked up a branch that had fallen off, and threw it back on the pile.

'I've asked you twice. How many fireworks have you got? I've got over two pounds' worth so far.'

Trust Norbert to start on about fireworks again. He knew I hadn't got any, 'cos we'd talked about it the day before. Barry didn't help either.

'I've got about two pounds' worth an' all, and my dad says he might get me some more.'

It wasn't fair. I bet if I had a dad, I'd have plenty of fireworks. It wasn't fair.

'My mum hasn't got mine yet.'

Norbert snorted. He's always doing that.

'Huh, I bet she won't get you none neither. She didn't last year. She wouldn't even let you come.'

'That was last year, wasn't it? She's getting me some this year.'

If only she was.

'Well, she'd better be quick, they're selling out. They've hardly got any left at Robinson's.'

Robinson's is the toy shop we all go to. Paul Robinson used to be in our class, but about two years back he was badly injured by a car. He doesn't go to our school any more. We see him sometimes in the holidays, but he doesn't seem to remember us.

'All right, all right, don't panic, she's getting them this morning, isn't she? She ordered them ages ago.'

I don't think Norbert believed me.

'Oh …How many is she getting you?'

He isn't half a pest, Norbert. He goes on and on.

'I don't know. I'll see when I get home at dinner time.'

When we got back to Belgrave Street, Tony was throwing stones up in the air, seeing how high he could get them, and Trevor was riding round on my bike. There were stones and bits of glass all over the place.

'Hey, Trevor, gerroff! You'll puncture it.'

I took my bike off him, and leaned it against a rusty oil drum. Tony started to load the wood on to the fire.

'You've been ages. What took you so long? It's nearly dinner time.'

Barry pointed at Norbert, who was throwing a branch on to the bonfire.

'Ask him, monkey-features. We spent twenty minutes trying to drag him off a tree!'

The branch rolled back and nearly hit Norbert in the face. He had another go, but it fell down again. While he was doing this, Trevor crept up behind him

He grinned at Tony, Barry and me and took a jumping jack out of his pocket. He lit it, threw it down by Norbert's feet and ran over to us. Norbert threw the branch up again and this time it stayed on top, and just as he was turning round with a cheer, the jumping jack went off and scared the living daylights out of him. We all laughed like anything, but Norbert didn't think it was funny.

'Who did that? I bet it was you.'

He ran towards me.

Trevor pulled another jumping jack out of his pocket and waved it at Norbert. Norbert went for him, but Trevor was too quick. Norbert chased after him and got him in a stranglehold. Somehow, Trevor got out of it.

'Blooming heck, Norbert, your hands don't half pong. What've you been up to?'

Barry and me laughed our heads off. So did Tony when we told him. Trevor didn't. He ran off home to have a wash. It was dinner time by now, so we all decided to go home. Except Norbert. He never goes home on a Saturday. His mum just gives him some money for his dinner, and he stays out all day. I wouldn't like it if my mum did that. I went over to get my bike.

'See you, Norbert.'

Norbert had gone back to throwing branches on to the fire.

'Yeah. Mebbe see you later.'

'Yeah, mebbe.'

I started walking with Tony and Barry, pushing my bike, but then I decided to cycle on ahead.

'I'd better get going. My mum'll be getting fish and chips.'

We always have fish and chips on a Saturday. I pedalled off just as Barry called after me.

'We'll come round after, have a look at your fireworks.'

Oh blimey! I braked.

'Oh, I've just remembered, I've got to go to my Auntie Doreen's with my mum. My Auntie Doreen is doing her hair. I've just remembered.'

That wasn't a complete lie. My mum was going to my Auntie Doreen's to have her hair done, but I didn't have to go with her. Ooh, why had I opened my big mouth earlier on? They're bound to find out my mum hadn't bought me any fireworks, 'specially when I don't turn up for the bonfire on Monday. Why was I the only one not to have my own fireworks?

I took a short cut through the park. You're not supposed to cycle in the park but it was a lot quicker. Anyway, there was hardly anybody about and the Park Ranger was most likely having his dinner. As I was going past the swings and slides, I saw this ginger-headed lad sitting on the kiddies' roundabout. It was going round very slowly, and he had a brown paper bag on his lap. Nobody else was about.

'Hey, you're not supposed to ride bikes in the park.'

He had a blooming cheek 'cos children over twelve aren't allowed on the swings and roundabouts, and this lad looked about fourteen.

'Well, you're not supposed to ride on the roundabouts if you're over twelve.'

He pushed himself round a bit faster with his foot.

'I know.'

He was a funny looking kid. I didn't know him, but I'd seen him around a few times. He was always on his own. I think he went to St Matthew's. He held up the paper bag.

'Do you want to see summat?'

I wondered what he'd got in it.

'No, I'm late for my dinner.'

He stopped the roundabout with his foot.

'I've got some fireworks in this bag.'

I got off my bike, and wheeled it over. He did have fireworks in his bag. Tons of them. Bangers, volcanoes, silver cascades, dive-bombers, jumping jacks, flowerpots – everything. Every firework you'd ever seen.

'Where did you get them?'

He looked at me.

'From a shop. Do you want to buy 'em?'

'I haven't got any money.'

That's when I thought of it. I must've been mad. I *was* mad.

'I'll swop my bike for them.'

He got off the roundabout.

'All right.'

He held out the paper bag and I took it, and he took my bike and cycled off.

I must've been off my head. I ran home clutching my

paper bag. I went in the back way, and hid my fireworks in the outhouse, behind the dustbin. I didn't enjoy my fish and chips at all. I kept thinking about my stupid swop. How could I have been so daft? I still had to go to the firework display at the Children's Hospital with my mum.

After dinner, my mum asked me if I wanted to go with her to my Auntie Doreen's.

'No, Mum, I said I might meet Tony and Barry.'

What I thought I'd do was go back to the park and try to find that lad and ask him to swop back. I mean, it wasn't a fair swop, was it?

'All right then love, but if you go anywhere on your bikes, be careful.'

I felt sick.

After my mum had gone, I went outside and got the bag of fireworks. I was looking at them in the front room when the door-bell rang. It couldn't have been my mum 'cos she's got a key, but I put the fireworks in a cupboard just in case and went to answer it. Norbert, Barry and Tony were standing there. Barry looked at the others, then looked at me with a kind of smile.

'We saw your mum going up Deardon Street. She said you were at home.'

I didn't say anything. I just looked at them. Norbert sniffed.

'Yeah. So we thought we'd come and look at your fireworks.'

Norbert grinned his stupid grin. I could've hit him – but I didn't have to.

'You don't believe I've got any fireworks, do you?' Tony and Barry didn't say anything. Norbert did. 'No!'

'I'll show you.'

I took them into the front room, and got the bag of fireworks out of the cupboard. I put them on the carpet, and we all kneeled round to have a look. They were really impressed – 'specially Norbert.

'Blooming hummer, did your mum buy you all these?'

'Course. I told you.'

Norbert kept picking one up after the other.

'But there's everything. Look at these divebombers. And look at the size of these rockets!'

Tony picked up an electric storm.

'These are great. They go on for ages.'

The three of them kept going through all the fireworks. They just couldn't believe it. I felt really chuffed.

'I'd better put them away now.'

Norbert had taken out a sparkler.

'I've never seen sparklers as big as these. Let's light one.'

'No, I'm putting them away now.'

I wanted to get rid of Barry, Tony and Norbert, and see if I could find that lad in the park. I'd proved I'd got my own fireworks now. I'd make up some excuse for not coming to the bonfire on Monday, but none of them could say I hadn't been given my own fireworks. None of them could say that, now.

'Go on, light a sparkler, just one. They're quite safe.'

Well, what harm could it do? Just one sparkler. I got the matches from the mantelpiece, and Norbert held it while I lit it. When it got going, I took hold of it, and we all sat round in a circle and watched it sparkle away. Suddenly, Tony screamed.

I looked down and saw lots of bright colours. For a split second I couldn't move. I was paralysed.

Suddenly, fireworks were flying everywhere. Bangers went off, rockets were flying. Sparks were shooting up to the ceiling. It was terrifying. Norbert hid behind the sofa, and Tony stood by the door, while Barry and me tried to put out the fireworks by stamping on them. I could hear Tony shouting, asking if he should fetch my mum.

'Yeah, get her, get her, she's at my Auntie Doreen's, get her!'

I don't know how long it took us, it could have been half an hour, it could have been five minutes, but somehow Barry and me managed to put all the fireworks out. The room was full of smoke, and we were coughing and choking like anything, and I couldn't stop myself from shaking, and even though I was sweating, I felt really cold.

As the smoke cleared, I saw my mum standing by the door, her hair wringing wet, and all I remember thinking was, that I wouldn't need an excuse for not going to the bonfire on Monday.

Notes on The Mile

This story addresses the theme of bullying, as in 'The Gang-hut' and 'The Holiday'. Yet as we see the narrator mature, we witness the way he is able to deal with this. His determination, so often used to defy his mother, is now channelled into a purposeful improvement of himself in sport. The way bullying can affect a students' academic success is also addressed, and despite his success on the sports field, the narrator lets his schoolwork deteriorate, to the disappointment of his mother, and himself.

What do you think?
Layton uses a story within a story – the beginning and end of 'The Mile' are set in the same place and time. See if you can pinpoint where the inner story begins and where we return to the outer story.

Questions
1. What do 'capricious and dilettante' mean?
2. What do you think of the language Mr Melrose uses on his English reports?
3. What has changed in the narrator's character and attitudes in this story?
4. What do these lines show about the narrator: 'I looked round ... I mean, we didn't go out with girls, because ... well ... we just didn't.'
5. Why do you think the narrator didn't finish the race?

Further activities
1. Research reading materials on bullying. Ask your teachers or librarian for suggestions. Then design a leaflet for new students at your school, giving them advice about bullying. Pay attention to layout. Be careful not to frighten your audience, but at the same time give realistic and useful advice. What procedure should pupils follow at your school?

2. In groups, using drama and poetry, prepare a 3-minute piece for assembly on bullying. Ask your teacher about poems, novels and stories dealing with bullying which you might use.

The Mile

What a rotten report. It was the worst report I'd ever had. I'd dreaded bringing it home for my mum to read. We were sitting at the kitchen table having our tea, but neither of us had touched anything. It was gammon and chips as well, with a pineapple ring. My favourite. We have gammon every Friday, 'cos my Auntie Doreen works on the bacon counter at the Co-op, and she drops it in on her way home. I don't think she pays for it.

My mum was reading the report for the third time. She put it down on the table and stared at me. I didn't say anything. I just stared at my gammon and chips and pineapple ring. What could I say? My mum looked so disappointed. I really felt sorry for her. She was determined for me to do well at school, and get my 'O' Levels, then get my 'A' Levels, then go to university, then get my degree, and then get a good job with good prospects ...

'I'm sorry Mum ...'

She picked up the report again, and started reading it for the fourth time.

'It's no good reading it again, Mum. It's not going to get any better.'

She slammed the report back on to the table.

'Don't you make cheeky remarks to me. I'm not in the mood for it!'

I hadn't meant it to be cheeky, but I suppose it came out like that.

111

'I wouldn't say anything if I was you, after reading this report!'

I shrugged my shoulders.

'There's nothing much I *can* say, is there?'

'You can tell me what went wrong. You told me you worked hard this term!'

I *had* told her I'd worked hard, but I hadn't.

'I did work hard, Mum.'

'Not according to this.'

She waved the report under my nose.

'You're supposed to be taking your "O" Levels next year. What do you think is going to happen then?'

I shrugged my shoulders again, and stared at my gammon and chips.

'I don't know.'

She put the report back on the table. I knew I hadn't done well in my exams 'cos of everything that had happened this term, but I didn't think for one moment I'd come bottom in nearly everything. Even Norbert Lightowler had done better than me.

'You've come bottom in nearly everything. Listen to this.'

She picked up the report again.

'Maths – Inattentive and lazy.'

I knew what it said.

'I know what it says, Mum.'

She leaned across the table, and put her face close to mine.

'I know what it says too, and I don't like it.'

She didn't have to keep reading it.

'Well, stop reading it then.'

My mum just gave me a look.

'English Language – he is capricious and dilettante. What does that mean?'

I turned the pineapple ring over with my fork. Oh heck, was she going to go through every rotten subject?

'Come on – English Language – Mr Melrose says you're "capricious and dilettante". What does he mean?'

'I don't know!'

I hate Melrose. He's really sarcastic. He loves making a fool of you in front of other people. Well, he could stick his 'capricious and dilettante', and his rotten English Language, and his set books, and his horrible breath that nearly knocks you out when he stands over you.

'I don't know what he means.'

'Well, you should know. That's why you study English Language, to understand words like that. It means you mess about, and don't frame yourself.'

My mum kept reading every part of the report over and over again. It was all so pointless. It wasn't as if reading it over and over again was going to change anything. Mind you, I kept my mouth shut. I just sat there staring at my tea. I knew her when she was in this mood.

'What I can't understand is how come you did so well at Religious Instruction? You got seventy-five per cent.'

I couldn't understand that either.

'I like Bible stories, Mum.' She wasn't sure if I was cheeking her or not. I wasn't.

'Bible stories? It's all I can do to get you to come to St Cuthbert's one Sunday a month with me and your Auntie Doreen.'

That was true, but what my mum didn't know was that the only reason I went was 'cos my Auntie Doreen slips me a few bob!

'And the only reason you go then is 'cos your Auntie Doreen gives you pocket money.'

'Aw, that's not true, Mum.'

Blimey! My mum's got eyes everywhere.

She put the report back into the envelope. Hurray! The Spanish Inquisition was over. She took it out again. Trust me to speak too soon.

'I mean, you didn't even do well at sport, did you? "Sport – He is not a natural athlete." Didn't you do *anything* right this term?'

I couldn't help smiling to myself. No, I'm not a natural athlete, but I'd done one thing right this term. I'd shown Arthur Boocock that he couldn't push me around any more. That's why everything else had gone wrong. That's why I was 'lazy and inattentive' at Maths, and 'capricious and dilettante' at English Language. That's why this last term had been so miserable, 'cos of Arthur blooming Boocock.

He'd only come into our class this year because he'd been kept down. I didn't like him. He's a right bully, but because he's a bit older and is good at sport and running and things, everybody does what he says.

That's how Smokers' Corner started.

114

Arthur used to pinch his dad's cigarettes and bring them to school, and we'd smoke them at playtime in the shelter under the woodwork classroom. We called it Smokers' Corner.

It was daft really. I didn't even like smoking, it gives me headaches. But I joined in 'cos all the others did. Well, I didn't want Arthur Boocock picking on me.

We took it in turns to stand guard. I liked it when it was my turn, it meant I didn't have to join in the smoking.

Smokers' Corner was at the top end of the playground, opposite the girls' school. That's how I first saw Janis. It was one playtime. I was on guard, when I saw these three girls staring at me from an upstairs window. They kept laughing and giggling. I didn't take much notice, which was a good job 'cos I saw Melrose coming across the playground with Mr Rushton, the Deputy Head. I ran into the shelter and warned the lads.

'Arthur, Tony – Melrose and Rushton are coming!'

There was no way we could've been caught. We knew we could get everything away before Melrose or Rushton or anybody could reach us, even if they ran across the playground as fast as they could. We had a plan you see.

First, everybody put their cigarettes out – not on the ground – with your fingers. It didn't half hurt if you didn't wet them enough. Then Arthur would open a little iron door that was in the wall next to the boiler house. Norbert had found it ages ago. It must've been there for years. Tony reckoned it was some sort of oven. Anyway, we'd empty our pockets and put all the cigarettes inside.

All the time we'd be waving our hands about to get rid of the smoke, and Arthur would squirt the fresh-air spray he'd nicked from home. Then we'd shut the iron door and start playing football or tig.

Melrose never let on why he used to come storming across the playground. He never said anything, but we knew he was trying to catch the Smokers – and he knew we knew. All he'd do was give us all a look in turn, and march off. But on that day, the day those girls had been staring and giggling at me, he did say something.

'Watch it! All of you. I know what you're up to. Just watch it. 'Specially you, Boocock.'

We knew why Melrose picked on Arthur Boocock.

'You're running for the school on Saturday, Boocock. You'd better win or I'll want to know the reason why.'

Mr Melrose is in charge of athletics, and Arthur holds the school record for the mile. Melrose reckons he could run for Yorkshire one day, if he trains hard enough.

I didn't like this smoking lark, it made me cough, gave me a headache, and I was sure we'd get caught one day.

'Hey Arthur, we'd better pack it in. Melrose is going to catch us one of these days.'

Arthur wasn't bothered.

'Ah you! You're just scared, you're yeller!'

Yeah, I was blooming scared.

'I'm not. I just think he's going to catch us.'

Then Arthur did something that really shook me. He took his right hand out of his blazer pocket – for a minute

I thought he was going to hit me – but he didn't. He put it to his mouth instead, and blew out some smoke. He's mad. He'd kept his cigarette in his hand – in his pocket – all the time. He's mad. I didn't say anything though. I was scared he'd thump me.

On my way home after school that day, I saw those girls. They were standing outside Wilkinson's sweetshop, and when they saw me they started giggling again. They're daft, girls. They're always giggling. One of them, the tallest, was ever so pretty though. The other two were all right, but not as pretty as the tall girl. It was the other two that were doing most of the giggling.

'Go on, Glenda, ask him.'

'No, you ask him.'

'No, you're the one who wants to know. You ask him.'

'Shurrup!'

The tall one looked as embarrassed as I felt. I could see her name written on her schoolbag – Janis Webster.

The other two were still laughing, and telling each other to ask me something. I could feel myself going red. I didn't like being stared at.

'Do you two want a photograph or summat?'

They giggled even more.

'No, thank you, we don't collect photos of monkeys, do we Glenda?'

The one called Glenda stopped laughing and gave the other one a real dirty look.

'Don't be so rude, Christine.'

Then, this Christine started teasing her friend Glenda.

'Ooh, just 'cos you like him, Glenda Bradshaw, just 'cos you fancy him.'

I started walking away. Blimey! If any of the lads came by and heard this going on, I'd never hear the end of it. The one called Christine started shouting after me.

'Hey, my friend Glenda thinks you're ever so nice. She wants to know if you want to go out with her.'

Blimey! Why did she have to shout so the whole street could hear? I looked round to make sure nobody like Arthur Boocock, or Norbert or Tony were about. I didn't want them to hear these stupid lasses saying things like that. I mean, we didn't go out with girls, because … well … we just didn't.

I saw the pretty one, Janis, pulling Christine's arm. She was telling her to stop embarrassing me. She was nice that Janis, much nicer than the other two. I mean, if I was forced to go out with a girl, you know if somebody said, 'You will die tomorrow if you don't go out with a girl', then I wouldn't have minded going out with Janis Webster. She was really nice.

I often looked out for her after that, but when I saw her, she was always with the other two. The one time I did see her on her own, I was walking home with Tony and Norbert and I'd pretended I didn't know her – even though she'd smiled and said hello. Course, I sometimes used to see her at playtime, when it was my turn to stand guard at Smokers' Corner. I liked being on guard twice as much now. As well as not having to smoke, it gave me a chance to see Janis. She was smashing. I couldn't get her out of my mind. I was always thinking about her, you know, having day-dreams. I was forever 'rescuing' her.

One of my favourite rescues was where she was being bullied by about half-a-dozen lads, not hitting her or anything, just mucking about. And one of them was always Arthur Boocock. And I'd go up very quietly and say, 'Are these lads bothering you?' And before she had time to answer, a fight would start, and I'd take them all on. All six at once, and it would end up with them pleading for mercy. And then Janis would put her hand on my arm and ask me to let them off ... and I would – that was my favourite rescue.

That's how the trouble with Arthur Boocock started.

I'd been on guard one playtime, and had gone into one of my 'rescues'. It was the swimming-bath rescue. Janis would be swimming in the deep end, and she'd get into trouble, and I'd dive in and rescue her. I'd bring her to the side, put a towel round her, and then walk off without saying a word. Bit daft really, because I can't swim. Not a stroke. Mind you, I don't suppose I could beat up six lads on my own either, 'specially if one of them was Arthur Boocock. Anyway, I was just pulling Janis out of the deep end when I heard Melrose shouting his head off.

'Straight to the Headmaster's study – go on, all three of you!'

I looked round, and I couldn't believe it. Melrose was inside Smokers' Corner. He'd caught Arthur, Tony and Norbert. He was giving Arthur a right crack over the head. How had he caught them? I'd been there all the time … standing guard … thinking about Janis … I just hadn't seen him coming…oh heck…

'I warned you, Boocock – all of you. Go and report to the Headmaster!'

As he was going past me, Arthur showed me his fist. I knew what that meant.

They all got the cane for smoking, and Melrose really had it in for Arthur even though he was still doing well at his running. The more Melrose picked on Arthur, the worse it was for me, 'cos Arthur kept beating me up.

That was the first thing he'd done after he'd got the cane – beat me up. He reckoned I'd not warned them about Melrose on purpose.

'How come you didn't see him? He's blooming big enough.'

'I just didn't.'

I couldn't tell him that I'd been day-dreaming about Janis Webster.

'He must've crept up behind me.'

Arthur hit me, right on my ear.

'How could he go behind you? You had your back to the wall. You did it on purpose, you yeller-belly!'

And he hit me again, on the same ear.

After that, Arthur hit me every time he saw me. Sometimes, he'd hit me in the stomach, sometimes on the back of my neck. Sometimes, he'd raise his fist and I'd think he was going to hit me, and he'd just walk away, laughing. Then he started taking my spending money. He'd say, 'Oh, you don't want that, do you?' and I'd say, 'No, you have it, Arthur.'

I was really scared of him. He made my life a misery. I dreaded going to school, and when I could, I'd stay at home by pretending to be poorly. I used to stick my fingers down my throat and make myself sick.

I suppose that's when I started to get behind with my school-work, but anything was better than being bullied by that rotten Arthur Boocock. And when I did go to school, I'd try to stay in the classroom at playtime, or I'd make sure I was near the teacher who was on playground duty. Course, Arthur thought it was all very funny, and he'd see if he could hit me without the teacher seeing – and he could.

Dinnertime was the worst because we had an hour free before the bell went for school dinners, and no one was allowed to stay inside. It was a school rule. That was an hour for Arthur to bully me. I used to try and hide but he'd always find me.

By now it didn't seem to have anything to do with him being caught smoking and getting the cane. He just seemed to enjoy hitting me and tormenting me. So I stopped going to school dinners. I used to get some chips, or a cornish pastie, and wander around. Sometimes, I'd go into town and look at the shops, or else I'd go in the park and muck about. Anything to get away from school and Arthur Boocock.

That's how I met Archie.

There's a running track in the park, a proper one with white lines and everything, and one day I spent all dinnertime watching this old bloke running round. That was Archie. I went back the next day and he was there again, running round and round, and I got talking to him.

'Hey mister, how fast can you run a mile?'

I was holding a bag of crisps, and he came over and took one. He grinned at me.

'How fast can *you* run a mile?'

I'd never tried running a mile.

'I don't know, I've never tried.'

He grinned again.

'Well, now's your chance. Come on, get your jacket off.'

He was ever so fast and I found it hard to keep up with him, but he told me I'd done well. I used to run with Archie every day after that. He gave me an old track-suit top, and I'd change into my shorts and pumps, and chase round the track after him. Archie said I was getting better and better.

'You'll be running for Yorkshire one of these days.'

I laughed and told him to stop teasing me. He gave me half an orange. He always did after running.

'Listen lad, I'm serious. It's all a matter of training. Anybody can be good if they train hard enough. See you tomorrow.'

That's when I got the idea.

I decided to go in for the mile in the school sports at the end of term. You had to be picked for everything else, but anybody could enter the mile.

There were three weeks to the end of term, and in that three weeks I ran everywhere. I ran to school. I ran with Archie every dinnertime. I went back and ran on the track after school. Then I'd run home. If my mum wanted anything from the shops, I'd run there. I'd get up really early in the mornings and run before breakfast. I was always running. I got into tons of trouble at school for not doing my homework properly, but I didn't care. All I thought about was the mile.

I had day-dreams about it. Always me and Arthur, neck and neck, and Janis would be cheering me on. Then I dropped Janis from my day-dreams. She wasn't important any more. It was just me and Arthur against each other. I was sick of him and his bullying.

Arthur did well at sports day. He won the high-jump and the long-jump. He was picked for the half-mile and the four-forty, and won them both. Then, there was the announcement for the mile.

'Will all those competitors who wish to enter the open mile, please report to Mr Melrose at the start.'

I hadn't let on to anybody that I was going to enter, so everybody was very surprised to see me when I went over in my shorts and pumps – especially Melrose. Arthur thought it was hilarious.

'Well, look who it is. Do you want me to give you half a mile start?'

I ignored him, and waited for Melrose to start the race. I surprised a lot of people that day, but nobody more than Arthur. I stuck to him like a shadow.

When he went forward, I went forward. If he dropped back, I dropped back. This went on for about half the race. He kept giving me funny looks. He couldn't understand what was happening.

'You won't keep this up. Just watch.'

And he suddenly spurted forward. I followed him, and when he looked round to see how far ahead he was, he got a shock when he saw he wasn't.

It was just like my day-dreams. Arthur and me neck and neck, the whole school cheering us on, both of us heading for the last bend. I looked at Arthur and saw the tears rolling down his cheeks. He was crying his eyes out. I knew at that moment I'd beaten him. I don't mean I knew I'd won the race. I wasn't bothered about that. I knew I'd beaten *him* – *Arthur*. I knew he'd never hit me again.

That's when I walked off the track. I didn't see any point in running the last two hundred yards. I suppose that's because I'm not a natural athlete.

'"Sport. He is not a natural athlete." Didn't you do anything right this term?'

Blimey! My mum was still reading my report. I started to eat my gammon and chips. They'd gone cold.

Notes on The Foursome

'The Foursome' clearly illustrates the growing maturity of the narrator and how Layton's stories move chronologically. The narrator has paid close attention to his clothes throughout *A Northern Childhood*, from 'The Balaclava Story' with his balaclava through to 'The Fib' with his embarrassment over his old-fashioned football kit. What is new, in 'The Foursome', is that he is now dressing to impress a girl as well as his friends.

What do you think?
Though the story is set in the 1950s and the fashions described are very different, consider the narrator's behaviour in preparing for his first date. Do you recognise any of his concerns? Do you think things have changed at all from what we see in this story?

Questions
1. Why do you think the narrator pretends to Barry that he is reluctant to go on the date?
2. What is different about the way the narrator speaks to his mother in this story?
3. Why does he decide to walk to the next bus stop and how does this fit in with what we have learnt about him previously?
4. What device does Layton use in the last line to structure his story?

Further activities
1. List the vocabulary in this story that reflects 1950s fashion. Find out the meaning of any unfamiliar words. You might find this information from older friends or relatives.

2. See if you can find any other words for fashionable clothes that older friends or relatives used to wear.

3. In groups make a list of words used in relation to modern teenagers' slang, clothes and fashion. Make your own dictionary to help people of older generations understand this language. Pay careful attention to the accuracy of your definitions.

The Foursome

I looked at myself in the long mirror. Fantastic! Yes, those new trousers were definitely it. Sixteen-inch bottoms and no turn-ups – boy, I couldn't wait for Barry to see them. Mind you, I'd wanted fifteen-inch bottoms, but there was no chance of that with my mum. She thinks anybody who wears drainpipes will end up in approved school.

'A teddy-boy – that's how you'll end up. It'll be velvet collars and long jackets next. Then those thick crepe shoes, I know.'

Blimey! Just 'cos one of my mates had ended up in a teddy-boy gang. I had teddy-boys morning, noon and night. Just watch, any second now and she'll come out with her Borstal line.

'You'll end up in Borstal, that's what'll happen to you.'

Told you.

'Don't be daft, mum!'

'Don't you talk to me like that – you may be going on for sixteen, but that's not too old for a quick slap.'

So, that's how it was. Sixteen-inch bottoms was the best I could do. But I knew there'd be more trouble when I brought the trousers home, and there were no turn-ups. I was right.

'But they're not finished. Where are the turn-ups?'

'There are no turn- ups.'

'I can see that. Where are they?'

'Turn-ups are out. They're old fashioned. This is the new style.'

Seeing as I'd bought the trousers out of my own money that I'd saved from my newspaper round, there wasn't much my mum could do about it.

'Well, you big jessie.'

And that was all she said.

But still, they did look great. I tilted the mirror forward a bit more, so that I could see how the tapered bottoms rested on my shoes. Terrific!

I was beginning to feel a bit nervous. This was the first date I'd ever had. The first proper date. Well, actually, it was a foursome. Barry had arranged it. He'd been on a couple of dates before, so he was quite experienced. We'd met these two girls at our school intersocial – we had one every Christmas with the girls' school nearby. It's the big event of the year, because it's the only time our school has anything to do with the girls' school. In fact, for a week before the intersocial, we had dancing-lessons in the main hall every lunchtime. You should have seen us. All the boys trying to learn to dance – together! I partnered Barry. We took it in turns to be the girl. By the end of the week, I could do a slow waltz!

At the intersocial, Barry had danced most of the time with this girl called Kath and he asked her out for the following Saturday, but she'd already arranged to go out with her best friend Valerie – and that's how the foursome was arranged: Barry and Kath, and me and Valerie. I'd had one dance with Valerie, so we sort of knew each other. She wasn't bad looking at all. In fact, going by standards in the girls' school, she was quite pretty.

Now which tie should I put on – my Slim Jim, or that fancy paisley one that I got from my Auntie Doreen for digging her garden? I think the Slim Jim – yeah, Jim's the him, I'll look great in that. As long as my mum doesn't see. To her, Slim Jim ties and bicycle chains go together. Now how do you do a Windsor? Across, under, across, under again – oh, I haven't enough tie left over, now. Across, under, under again, back across – and you get a big fat mess. Right, once more, and if I don't get it right this time I'm not going. Across, under, under again, back across and third time lucky – a perfect Windsor knot, and just enough left over to tuck in my trousers.

You handsome brute! I liked looking in this mirror. My spots didn't look too bad. Who are you kidding – you look like the before bloke in that acne advert. Oh, how is it you always look your worst when it matters the most? Ah well, Valerie knows what I look like.

My collar didn't look too bad, considering I'd had to use matchsticks instead of whale-bones. I'd been thinking about this date all week. In fact, I couldn't think about anything else. Now I kept wondering whether to go or not. Well, course I wanted to go – I wouldn't miss it for anything. Mind you, I hadn't let on to Barry that I was keen. I made out I was doing him a favour when he asked me.

'Look, Kath'll only go out with me, if you'll take out her friend – go on, take her out, she's not bad looking y'know.'

I didn't have to think twice. I liked her.

'I don't know, Barry, I'm not right keen.'

'Oh, well, if you're not – I suppose I'll have to ask Norbert Lightowler.'

'All right, Barry, but only because you are my best friend.'

'You're a good lad. I'll fix it up then.'

And he arranged to meet them outside the Odeon at quarter to eight.

Now for a touch of after-shave – not that I had anything to shave. I'd only used this stuff once before – when I went to our Maureen's birthday party. Maureen's my cousin. That was a waste of time an' all. The oldest girl there was only thirteen – and that was our Maureen. What a lousy party. A load of giggling school-girls all asking me what kind of perfume I used. At least Valerie would appreciate the exhilarating freshness, the new experience in aftershave. I slapped some on my face – ooh, smashing stuff this. It certainly was a new experience. I looked in the mirror. What it did was make my pimples look healthy. After a few seconds, the stinging stopped, and I must say, it *was* quite an exhilarating freshness.

I just had my hair to do now, and I'd be ready. Barry had a great hairstyle – a Tony Curtis. They were all the rage. He could only have it like that at weekends though, 'cos at our school they're banned by the Headmaster. Barry says that he's jealous 'cos he's bald. He might be right, I don't know. It just seems to me that whenever you try to look smart or be a bit different, you're suddenly branded as a hooligan and everybody's telling you you're half-way to Borstal. It seems daft to me.

I couldn't have a Tony Curtis anyway, my hair just won't go that way. Barry says it's 'cos I've got a double-crown. So I do it with a parting and a big quiff at the front. The trouble is, I keep getting a tuft of hair sticking up at the back. It's my double-crown I suppose. Barry never has that trouble. He's invented a special hair lotion – sugar and water mixed. It makes his hair as stiff as a board.

Hey, what time was it? I hadn't been watching the time at all. I went to the top of the stairs.

'Hey, Mum, what time is it?'

'Eh?'

'I said what time is it?'

'Come down here.'

I don't know! My old mum! She's getting deaf in her old age.

'What's wrong, are you going deaf?'

'Y'what!'

I knew why she couldn't hear. She was running the tap in the kitchen. It's always the same when you're in a hurry.

'Look Mum, all I wanted was the time.'

'Oh … ten to seven.'

I could see that for myself now, from the kitchen clock. What a fantastic clock as well. It's one of those like a frying pan that you hang on the wall, and it has a smiling face painted on it. It had hung above the fireplace for as long as I could remember. My mum was very fond of it. She says it's never been a minute out since she's had it.

'Yes, ten to seven. It's dead right that is. It's never been out since I've had it.'

Ten to seven. I'd better get a move on, I was supposed to be meeting Barry at seven down in town. We'd arranged to meet early.

'Tarah Mum, I've got to go.'

I thought I'd got out without my mum saying anything, but that would've been too much to hope for.

'Hey, just a minute.'

Oh dear, here we go.

'Er, what Mum?'

I tried to make it sound as if I had no idea what she wanted.

'Er, what do you want?'

'Where do you think you're going dressed like that?'

Oh, if she started an argument now, I'd never get away.

'Dressed like what, Mum?'

'Don't act the innocent with me, you know what I mean.

'No, I don't.'

I could see that if I wasn't careful, I was going to be here for ages.

'Those tight trousers – and that bootlace round your neck.'

She meant my Slim Jim.

'That's my Slim Jim.'

'And why don't you get your hair cut?'

I knew it was best not to argue, but I couldn't stop myself.

'What's wrong with my hair?'

My mum was really getting into her stride now.

'Why don't you use your tie for a hair-ribbon? And what's that smell, have you been at my perfume?'

'Don't be daft. It's my after-shave.'

'Oh, I see. Well, when you're in court with all your other teddy-boy friends, don't you come running to me.'

'Oh, I'm off.'

And I went before she could say anything, though I could hear her shouting after me.

'And be careful!'

I don't know, me and my mum, we always seemed to be squabbling these days.

I didn't know whether to wait for a bus, or start walking to the next stop – it's a penny cheaper from there. I decided to walk, and of course, when I was right between the stops, a bus went past, so I ended up walking all the way. I was about a quarter of an hour late when I got to town, and Barry was already waiting for me.

'Hey, where've you been? I've been standing here freezing for quarter of an hour.'

'Sorry, Barry. I had a bit of a doo-dah with my mum.'

I could see Barry looking at my new trousers.

'Hey, are those your new pants?'

'Yes. What do you think?'

'They're great, kiddo, great!'

Barry had some new trousers on as well. A sort of bronzy colour.

'Yours are new an' all, aren't they?'

'Yeah – first time on. What are your bottoms?'

'Sixteens. What's yours?'

'Fifteens.'

Huh, Barry was lucky! His mum and dad let him wear just what he wanted.

'I wanted fifteens, but my mum wouldn't let me.'

As we weren't meeting Kath and Valerie outside the Odeon till quarter to eight, we had about twenty minutes to kill, so we went for a coffee. It was a new coffee bar that had only been open a couple of weeks. I'd never been before, but Barry had.

It was quite full inside, so Barry told me to look for somewhere to sit while he got the coffees.

'What do you want?'

'Tea, please.'

I wasn't too fond of coffee.

'You can't have tea in a coffee bar.'

'Course you can.'

'Oh, all right.'

While I was looking around, I saw a couple of people I knew – one of them was a teacher at our school. Funny, you don't expect to find people like that in a coffee-bar. I saw two seats on their own near the window. I signalled to Barry and he followed me over.

'Here's your tea.'

'Ta.'

It was the funniest cuppa I'd ever had.

'Hey, Barry, I asked for tea.'

'It is tea. It's lemon tea. That's what you drink in coffee bars.'

'Oh.'

We didn't take long over our drinks 'cos it wasn't far off quarter to eight, and we were just going when Barry said he wanted to tell me something.

'Yeah, what is it?'

'Well, just one thing. Err …when we get inside the pictures   …
err …if I start kissing Kath, you'll have to start kissing Valerie.'

'Y'what?'

I thought he was kidding at first, but he looked very serious.

'Y'see it's like that on a foursome.'

'Well, what if she doesn't want to kiss me?'

'Course she will. You just follow me, you'll be all right. Here, have a peppermint.'

I must say, Barry was very confident. I didn't like the sound of it at all. I mean I hardly knew her. How would I know if she wanted to kiss me? Oh, heck.

The town-hall clock was just striking quarter to as we got to the Odeon. I could see Kath waiting for us – but I couldn't see Valerie.

'Hey, Barry. Mine hasn't turned up.'

'Course she has. She's probably inside getting some sweets.'

Kath saw us coming and came to meet us. I left all the talking to Barry.

'Hi, Kath, where's Valerie, inside?'

She gave me a funny sort of look, and I knew what was coming. She'd probably gone and got chicken-pox, mumps, or something like that.

'She isn't here. It's her dad.'

Her dad? What's her dad got to do with it? This was too much for me.

'What's her dad got to do with it?'

'He won't let her come. He says she can't go out with *you* – 'cos you're a teddy-boy!'

Notes on The Exam

The finality of exams and leaving school is reflected in this, the final story of *A Northern Childhood*. The narrator's concern about his family and friends is consistent with what we have already learnt about him, however this time his poor concentration on his school work has far-reaching consequences.

What do you think?
As you read, consider this story as the last in *A Northern Childhood*. How is it an appropriate end to the book?

Questions
1. What has happened to the following characters we met earlier: Barry, Norbert and Tony?
2. 'It's ridiculous, I'm nearly eighteen and still at school.' What advice would you offer the narrator at this point in the story?
3. What is impressive about Tony's achievements?
4. What has the narrator realised about his mother, that distracts him during his exam?
5. Discuss the importance of the last line of this story, and the book as a whole.

Further activities
1. Now you've finished the book, write your own review of it on one of the following internet sites:
   http://www.uk.bol.com
   http://amazon.co.uk

   Search for *A Northern Childhood* and then click on 'Write your own review'.

   You can also find a place to write book reviews on 'Stories from the Web' at http://ukoln.ac.uk.

2. You might also like to read what famous writers have said about themselves and their own writing at the 'Writers Online' internet site. You can even send them your work to look at:
   http://www.yearofreading.org.uk/reading/writers/index.html

The Exam

I looked at the exam paper. 'Northern Universities Joint Matriculation Board. History – Advanced Level.' Bit like seeing an old friend – no, an old enemy, that'd be more like it. We'd been doing practice exam papers like these for eighteen months now – and I'd grown to hate them. Well, this time it was the real thing. The climax of seven years at grammar school. I had to finish this paper. It wasn't just a rehearsal for the big day. No excuses like:

'Well, sir, I thought this time I'd just concentrate on the Napoleonic Wars, sir' – which translated meant, 'What a lousy paper! There was only one question I could do – the Napoleonic Wars.'

I couldn't bring myself to read this real paper, at first. I kept thinking about my mum. I kept thinking about what had happened the other day. Why should a little thing like that have made such a difference? But it did. Nothing seemed important any more.

I looked round the hall. The school had hired it specially, 'cos there has to be three feet space between each desk – the school hall would have been big enough for two feet space, but not for three. This hall belonged to the Territorial Army, and every now and again we could hear what sounded like five hundred men marching by. Usually, we sit our exams at the Mechanics Institute, but this year somebody had forgotten to book it up, and the Amateur Operatic and Dramatic Society had beaten us to it, and were rehearsing 'The Dancing Years' there.

Before the exam had started, Mr Holdsworth, the invigilator – he's the woodwork master at our school, and he taught me about five years ago, but I don't think he knows me from Adam now – anyway, he told us all not to take any notice of the noises outside. He didn't tell us that half the army would be on the move. I think I prefer 'The Dancing Years'!

As I was looking round, I could see all the other lads engrossed in their work. I could see Norbert Lightowler picking his nose. I had to laugh to myself. For seven years I'd watched Norbert Lightowler pick his nose. He can't help it. He doesn't know he's doing it. It must help him concentrate, I suppose. I mean, some people bite their nails when they're concentrating, and some people chew gum. Well, Norbert, he picks his nose.

I remember when we first came to grammar school, one of the teachers shouted out, 'Wrong way home, Lightowler'. We didn't know what he meant, of course, but everybody soon realised – except Norbert. After a while nobody noticed any more. We just left him alone.

It's funny really. Out of our crowd there's only Norbert and me still here. Barry left even before 'O' levels. He should never have gone to a grammar school – his mum and dad weren't at all pleased when he passed his scholarship. Too much expense they said. Actually, they didn't believe him at first. They said it wasn't possible. You couldn't blame them, either. Nobody thought Barry'd get to grammar school. Anyway he left before he was sixteen. He's working in a butcher's shop now. Doing all right, too. I saw him the other day. He's assistant manager. Reckons he'll be manager when they open a new branch.

'I'm telling you, kid, when I'm managing this branch I'll be knocking up fourteen or fifteen quid a week basic – and then there's my commission.'

I told him about prospects and future and all that. You know, like my mum tells me. But I didn't convince him. I didn't even convince myself.

'What are you talking about, future and prospects? Nineteen and managing my own shop nearly. That isn't a bad future, is it?'

I had to agree with him.

'I mean what do you do at weekends? How much money do you have to spend?'

I told him about my grocery round.

'I do my grocery round at Atkinson's. I get fifteen bob for that.'

'Fifteen bob!'

'Yes, and my mum gives me another fifteen bob.'

'Not much, is it – thirty bob.'

'It lasts me!'

Does it heckers like last me. By Thursday, I always have to cadge off my mum.

'Well, all I can say is that leaving school was the best thing that's happened to me.'

As I was reading the exam paper, I started thinking that leaving school would've been the best thing to happen to me, too. It's ridiculous, I'm nearly eighteen and still at school. Barry's right. It's okay to talk about the future and prospects – but what about the present? Life's just passing me by.

Norbert was still picking his nose – only twice as much now, 'cos he was writing faster. Oh, I'd better get on with the exam, I suppose. I started reading through, and ticked the questions I thought I could answer.

But honest! I reckon one of the biggest mistakes of my life was passing the scholarship to grammar school. I'd've been all right if I hadn't gone to the grammar. I'd've left school at fifteen, got a regular job, and by now, I'd have some cash in my pocket. No, I don't mean that – but it does all seem a waste of time. Same with these 'A' levels. I'm not bothered about going to university. But my mum talks to me about prospects and future, and how she's going to work hard so I can go on studying. I can't turn round and tell her she's wasting her time, 'cos… well, she's my mum. She's always right. At least, I used to think so, anyway – till the other day.

I mean, if it hadn't been for my mum, I'd've jacked this lot in ages ago – like Barry and Tony. Mind you, with Tony it was a bit different. He wanted to stay at school.

Tony was always cleverer than me. Even at primary school, he was always top of the class. The brain of the school we used to call him. We were in the same class at the grammar – and he was always in the top three. He was good at sport as well. Not like Arthur Holdroyd who's good at exams – and that's all. It sounds rotten, but I can't think of anybody who likes Arthur Holdroyd – not even the teachers. He's very clever – but slimy with it. I can't even imagine his own family liking him. Or like Dennis Gower. Now he used to be brilliant at sports – cricket, soccer, running, jumping – absolutely terrific – but he was as thick as the custard we have at our school dinners. Mind you, if I had the choice – I mean to be like Arthur Holdroyd or Dennis Gower – I'd rather be like Dennis any day.

Now Tony had the best of both worlds. He got seven 'O' Levels in one go, but then he had to leave. His mum and dad couldn't afford to keep him on. I don't think they realised how clever he was. Anyway, there's all his brothers and sisters – three brothers and two sisters, all younger than him – so you can see, he had to leave school to bring a bit more money in. I remember, he left in the July and we both went camping for a week, in the Lake District. Then he started work the day after we got back. He went as an apprentice engineer to Bulmer's.

Bulmer's is a big engineering works near us – his dad works there an' all, and his mum goes in part-time, cleaning. Quite a family affair really. I sometimes kid him on about it.

'Get a few more of your family at Bulmer's, and you might as well move in.'

'No need for that. There's talk of them transferring the works to our house.'

That's not far off the truth either. It's a right tip is their house. Thousands of kids running round with no clothes on, or perhaps just a vest or an odd sock. His mum shouting at everybody – mostly at his dad, who never takes any notice, 'cos he's too busy working out which horses are going to lose that day. Oh, it's a right blooming hole is that house. And Tony used to sit at the table amongst the bread and jam and condensed milk doing his homework. I used to wonder how he could do any work at all with that racket going on.

'How the hell you can do your homework in that blooming row, I don't know.'

'Oh, it doesn't bother me – I just get on with it.'

And every exam he'd come out in the top three. It's a shame he had to leave school, he'd have done really well. Mind you, he's doing all right now. He'll be finishing his apprenticeship soon, and then, like Barry, he'll be knocking up quite a good wage. He's engaged an' all – but she's decided she wants to wait till he finishes his apprenticeship before they get married, and he's agreed.

'Y'see, once I'm qualified we'll be able to save about five or six pounds a week for a deposit on a house.'

'Yes, but don't you think you're a bit young to get married?'

'I'll be going on for twenty – that's not young these days.'

Y'see, it seems daft. I'm still at school and there's Tony arranging to get married. I've agreed to be his best man.

Oh, dear! Hey, c'mon, I better get started on this paper. Question number one, 'Walpole was the first Prime Minister of this country. Comment.'

What a daft question! 'Walpole was the first Prime Minister of this country. Comment!' So what! Walpole *was* the first Prime Minister of this country! *Walpole* was the first Prime Minister of this country!

Good God! Norbert's actually using a handkerchief.

I don't think I've ever seen that before.

Norbert Lightowler is actually using a handkerchief! Comment! Poor old Norbert. Y'know, his dad makes him do the pools every week, and if he doesn't win, he gets thumped. That's what makes me feel guilty. I'm really the only one who's got it easy. My mum's perfect.

At least, that's what I used to think. I mean, what she did the other day shouldn't make such a difference. It wasn't stealing – it was harmless really. It was nothing.

We'd been out shopping at Atkinson's – where I do my grocery round – and when we got outside, my mum looked all pleased with herself.

'Hey, Mr Atkinson gave me ten shillings too much in the change.'

And that was it. She just put it in her purse and forgot about it. And all I could think was, if it had been me, she'd have sent me straight back. But she just dismissed it. I never said anything to her, but everything seemed different from then on.

Suddenly, Mr Holdsworth shouted something out.

'All right, boys, you can stop writing now.'

I didn't know what the hell was going on at first, and then it dawned on me – the exam was over! I looked at my watch. Blimey, I'd been day-dreaming for three hours – three hours! Mr Holdsworth came round, collecting up the papers. He nearly passed out when he saw mine.

'Well, I'll go to Sheffield!' And he just stood there looking at me.

I couldn't think of anything to say, so I mumbled something about it being a difficult paper, and that I'd been unlucky with the questions.

When my mum asked me that night how I'd got on, I just told her I didn't finish the paper.

That didn't bother her.

'Oh, you'll pass with flying colours – I know you will. You'll be at the university soon…'

I've been working at Bulmer's for three months now. My mum was very upset at first when I didn't get into university, but she was all right after a while. It's not too bad at Bulmer's – it's a change from school, anyway. I don't see much of Tony, though. Y'see, I'm in the office. I'm a white-collar worker. My mum's very proud of me.

Further reading

Bill's New Frock by Anne Fine (Longman, 1992)
Bill wakes up to find he's turned into a girl. He's forced to wear a pink dress and is not allowed to play football. In this lively comedy Anne Fine explores how girls and boys are treated differently.

Buddy by Nigel Hinton (Puffin, 1994)
A book which looks at the confusions of being a teenager in a thoughtful and often amusing way. Buddy is embarrassed by his father who is more interested in dreaming of his teddy-boy youth, listening to old records and a life of crime, than taking on the real responsibilities of parenthood.

Boy by Roald Dahl (Puffin, 1995)
The famous author's autobiography contains tales of his own childhood. He describes nearly losing his nose in a motor car accident, putting a mouse in the terrifying Mrs Pratchett's sweet jar and the pleasures of testing chocolates for Cadbury's. A lively and humorous set of tales, all of which are true.

Going Solo by Roald Dahl (Puffin, 1988)
The second book detailing Dahl's life, starting from his employment as a young man in Tanzania through to his service in the Royal Air Force during the Second World War.

The Demon Headmaster by Gillian Cross (Puffin, 1995)
From the very first day at school Dinah can tell that her new school is far from normal. Here are children that obey all the rules, follow the Headmaster's orders without question and act almost like robots. She and her friends form a gang, with a meeting place, password and mission, as in 'The Gang-hut' and attempt to overthrow the Demon Headmaster.

Badger on the Barge by Janni Howker (Walker, 1996)
A book of stories which focus on the relationships between young and old. Like *A Northern Childhood,* these are set in the north of England.

Flour Babies by Anne Fine (Longman, 2000)
A lively book which, like George Layton's, focuses on the settings of home and school. A group of boys, who are not academically bright, undertake a project to look after a sack of flour to learn about the responsibility of parenthood. The project allows Simon Martin, the central character, to think about the demands his mother has accepted in bringing him up, and the reasons why his father might have left him when he was young.

A Roald Dahl Selection (Longman, 2000)
A superb collection of nine stories by one of the outstanding storytellers of the twentieth century. A crazy bet, the perfect murder, painful memories of school – Dahl's plots hold us enthralled until the final unexpected twist.

Twisters (Longman, 2000)
This gripping collection of short stories from a wide variety of cultures and different eras ranges from Chaucer's 'The Pardoner's Tale' to Maupassant's 'The Necklace', from 'The Monkey Paw' which makes wishes come true to the Russian folk tale where gypsies bring a man back from the dead.

Programme of study

Passage 1: The Gang-hut

From 'We had lots of things in the gang-hut' to '"Why did he do it?"' (Pages 66–73)

Word

In this early story, the narrator's language of description is rather undeveloped. Read the passage from 'We had lots of things in the gang-hut' to 'two candles which were kept for emergency.' (Pages 66–7)

1. The narrator says of the hut: 'I thought it looked nice'. Consider more interesting synonyms for the word 'nice'. How many can you think of that would make the description more interesting? You might like to use a paper or electronic thesaurus to add to your ideas.

2. Copy out the common nouns in this passage that list what is in the gang-hut. Add adjectives which convey an accurate picture of how you imagine the gang-hut. Make an effort to choose appropriate, but thought-provoking words.

Sentence

Most of this novel consists of recounted stories, where the narrator tells of his experience and observations. Such texts usually contain some of the following types of writing:
- description of setting or characters
- reported speech
- personal opinion
- thoughts and feelings
- factual information.

Find a quotation from the passage that you think is a good example of each of these types of writing.

Text

The description of the gang-hut, as with the rest of the novel, is given from the viewpoint of the narrator. Re-read the passage from 'We had lots of things in the gang-hut' to '"Why did he do it?"' and consider the answer to that final question. Think carefully about Barry's character and motivation.

The following quotations might help you think about his motivation:

(a) 'Barry's voice suddenly became deeper, and rather bossy.
    "Well, if you'd attended the last gang meeting, you would have known what password!"'
(b) 'Barry always got things his way, pushing his weight around and telling us how much better he did things than we did.'
(c) 'Barry was in Standard Four and was going in for his scholarship in December. Tony and me were only in Standard Three.'
(d) 'There was also a picture … Barry didn't like it 'cos he thought it looked soppy.'
(e) 'Barry just lost his temper then and threw the potato on the floor.'

Write Barry's diary entry explaining how he felt about his friends and the gang-hut and why he vandalised it. Think about the events of the passage from his viewpoint rather than the narrator's.

Passage 2: The Long Walk
From 'It was very dark and all you could see was a little speck of light' (page 42) to the end of the story.

You will notice that there is much more descriptive language in this story than in the rest of *A Northern Childhood*. At the end of these activities you may have some ideas about why George Layton uses these techniques in this particular story.

Word

This story looks back at the events in the narrator's memory, deals with the present in the story and looks to the future as grandad thinks about what will happen to him.

1. Look through the following sentences from the first section of the passage up to 'And we did' (page 42). Decide whether each sentence describes the past, present or future.

One of the most important functions of a verb is to indicate the time at which an action takes place, so you may find it helpful to underline the active verb in the sentence. Look at the time line to help you.

Past time   Present time   Future time

(a) '"You go first, Grandad."'
(b) '"Here you are. These are for the journey. Off we go for the last time."'
(c) '"I mean it'll soon be winter, won't it. Come on."'
(d) 'We went down the steps.'
(e) '"Grandad, there are a hundred and fifteen steps, there."'
(f) 'I ran over to have a look at it and Grandad followed me.'
(g) '"It's like a house isn't it, Grandad?"'

2. Do you find the present tense more often in the dialogue or in the narrative? Can you think of a reason for this?

Sentence

This story shows the links between opposites; young and old, boy and man, past and present.

1. Finish off the sentences below, giving your own opinions about the characters. In your sentences try to reflect the balance and opposites that are shown in the story.

(a) While grandad is an old man …

(b) Though the young boy hates wearing clogs …

(c) Despite the fact that the mother is sometimes portrayed as harsh and strict in the book …

(d) Although there is a large age gap between the narrator and his grandfather …

(e) Whilst everyone else in the house is shocked when the grandfather dies …

(f) Though the mother realises her father is old …

(g) Whereas the narrator understands that his grandfather is going to die, …

2. Underline the subordinator in each of the above sentences.

Text

1. Look at the passage where the narrator eats his sandwiches, from 'And we did' to 'I wanted to go home' (pages 43–44). The writer appeals to our senses to help us imagine the situation. Imagine you are the narrator. What can you smell, touch, see, hear and taste?

2. Write your own piece of description entitled 'A place that is special to me'. It will help if you write it while you are sitting in that place, whether it is inside or outside. You will need to:

- Remember to appeal to your readers' senses.
- Look carefully at your surroundings, noticing the tiniest detail.
- See if you can include some interesting similes to help your reader imagine what you are describing.
- Often your mood affects what you notice – think carefully about how you are feeling and try to convey your mood to your reader through what you choose to describe.

Passage 3: The Mile

From 'What a rotten report' to '"It means you mess about and don't frame yourself"' (pages 111–113); and from 'Arthur hit me, right on my ear' (page 120) to the end.

Word

'"That's why you study the English language, to understand words like that."' (Page 113)

One way of being able to understand more words is to be able to break them down into their component parts. Knowledge of *prefixes* will help you in this. A prefix is a sound placed at the beginning of a word to form a new word. The word prefix itself contains the prefix *pre-* which means 'before' or 'in front of'. So pre-fix means to put a word before another.

1. Think of as many words as you can beginning with the prefix *pre-*. Write out their meanings. You might want to use a dictionary to help you.

2. Copy out the following table and add another example to column 4:

Prefix	Meaning	Example 1	Example 2
semi	half	semitone	
multi	many	multipurpose	
contra	against	contraindication	
re	again	retell	
fore	before	foretell	
sub	under	subterranean	
mis	wrong	misspelling	
tri	three	tricycle	
de	downward	descent	

3. Have a go at some of the games with prefixes and suffixes on the Wild World of Words Challenges pages at the Stockport LEA Internet Site, which has lots of ideas for literacy work at: http://webserv1.stockportmbc.gov.uk/curriculum/english/english.htm

Sentence

'Even Norbert Lightowler had done better than me' (Page 112). Look at the report below for Norbert Lightowler.

1. Underline the main topic of each sentence. You can then see the categories that the teacher reports on.

2. Underline three finite verbs in the report. What tense is it written in?

3. Is the written style of the report formal or informal?

Norbert has made some progress this term and has particularly improved in his reading skills. He is now able to read aloud fluently and I am pleased to see that he is able to choose himself appropriate books from the library. His written skills are still a little weak, and he needs to concentrate particularly on using full stops. His speaking and listening skills have also improved. At times, however, Norbert's behaviour is disruptive and he is distracted into amusing his friends when he should be concentrating on the lesson. His concentration is particularly poor during time given over to individual written work. I was particularly pleased with Norbert's recent piece of writing based around Bonfire Night, where he wrote a lively and imaginative story.

His targets for next term are to continue to develop his personal reading at home and to focus on full stops in written work.

4. Now write the report you imagine the narrator received. Remember to cover the appropriate categories of information, write in the correct tense and adopt an appropriate style.

Text

Re-read the stories 'The Holiday', 'The Gang-hut' and 'The Mile' and consider the topic of bullying. Look at the following essay title and complete the writing frame below for a mini-essay. Remember to develop each point made in the topic sentence, choose a quotation and then comment on it. The first paragraph after the introduction is done for you.

Discuss the portrayal of bullies and bullying in *A Northern Childhood* and what the theme reveals about the narrator.

(a) *Introduction*: *A Northern Childhood* is by George Layton. It is set in the north of England in the 1950s and shows a boy growing up. The earliest of the three stories that deal with bullying are 'The Holiday', 'The Gang-hut' and 'The Mile'. We can see how the narrator grows up and deals with bullying.

(b) The first bully we are introduced to is Gordon Barraclough. The narrator is put into his tent during camp which ruins the whole holiday for him. He says: 'he's a right bully and he gets everybody on his side 'cos they're all scared of him.' Gordon and his gang make the narrator sleep near the door of the tent and he gets wet when it rains. They also throw his clothes around and laugh at the fact that he has brought a suitcase.

(c) The bullying in the second story consists of …

(d) The final bully we meet is …

(e) In 'The Holiday' the narrator does not really deal with the bullying directly. His reaction is to …

(f) In 'The Gang-hut' the narrator reacts to the leader of the gang by …

(g) The final story is very different and we can see how the narrator is able to tackle the bully with confidence and thoughtfulness ...

(h) Overall, I think the portrayal of bullying in *A Northern Childhood* is ...

Glossary

The Balaclava Story

9   **balaclava:** tight woollen hat that covers the head and neck with holes for the eyes and mouth

       curse: evil wished on someone

       liable to: likely to

10   **daft:** silly, foolish

11   **handicraft:** a subject involving art and craft work

       goose-gogging: picking gooseberries

12   ***Noddy in Toyland*:** a book for young children written by Enid Blyton

13   **Man Friday:** a character from the book *Robinson Crusoe*

14   **tarah:** (slang) goodbye

15   **culprit:** the guilty person

       lousy: bad, useless

The Christmas Party

21   **Ludo:** traditional board game

23   **Polony:** a dry sausage of half-cooked meat

24   **spiteful:** wanting to hurt others

25   **Bridlington:** a coastal town in north-east England

26   **wireless:** an old word for radio

27   **sixpence:** an old English coin worth two and a half pence

       fibber: liar

       Did she heckers-like: (slang) I don't believe you, no she did not

       'owt: shortened form of 'nowt' meaning nothing

       sodden: heavy with water, completely wet through

29   **quarrelling:** arguing

30   **snicket:** a small alley

33   **grace:** a short prayer before or after a meal

34   **Aspic:** savoury meat flavoured jelly

The Long Walk

37   **clogs:** traditional northern wooden shoes

38   **windcheater:** anorak

39   **trackless:** the grandad uses this word in reference to old fashioned buses which ran on tracks

        conductor: the person on a bus who collects the fares

42   **Black Hole of Calcutta:** a dark and terrible place. The phrase comes from a dark cell in an Indian prison in Calcutta where, in 1756, 146 British prisoners were held. The next morning only 23 were found alive.

        barge: a long boat (or narrow boat) on a canal

43   **lock-gates:** gates built in canals to control the water level

44   **fit as a fiddle:** healthy and energetic

The Holiday

47   **clout:** hit

        boarding house: cheap holiday lodging house

48   **dislocated:** an injury where you knock a bone out of position

        RSPCC: the narrator is confusing the NSPCC (National Society for the Prevention of Cruelty to Children) and the RSPCA (Royal Society for the Prevention of Cruelty to Animals)

49   **Key-of-the-door, old-age-pension, legs-eleven, clickety-click:** phrases used when the numbers are called in a bingo game

        spam fritters: a kind of ham fried in batter

        deposit: money given as a promise of commitment

50   **playing the goat:** fooling around

        macaroni cheese: cheese pasta meal

51   *Drake's Drum*: title of a poem

52   **hammock:** hanging bed made out of rope

        Slung a' tween: thrown or stretched between

55   **Old Testament:** the older half of the Bible

Ten Commandments: the 10 laws in the Bible told to Moses by God

Bloomin' hummer: (slang) expression of surpise

56   **recite:** to read a poem aloud

59   **schedules:** lists

60   **marquee:** a huge tent

It's quite deceiving: from the outside it looks smaller than it really is.

61   **natter:** talk, chat

fuddy-duddies: old and uninteresting people

The Gang-hut

63   **password:** secret word needed to gain entry

Scarborough: a coastal resort in Yorkshire

aye: (dialect) yes

64   **I'd cheeked my Auntie Doreen off:** (slang) I'd been cheeky to my Auntie Doreen

65   **pushing his weight around:** being bossy and controlling

Standard Four: equal to junior school Year 6

scholarship: exam taken to enter an academic school

grammar school: the type of school children went to if they passed the scholarship exam

66   **Robin Hood:** historical figure who is said to have lived in Sherwood Forest in the fourteenth century. It is said that he stole from the rich and gave to the poor.

67   **nosy parkers:** very nosy people

68   **seal:** a special mark or symbol

69   **reluctant:** unwilling

birthmark: a natural mark on someone's body that they are born with

73   **matinee:** film screening during the day

wrecked: destroyed

The Firework Display

95   **Park Ranger:** person who maintains and supervises a park

hoist: lift

96   **You're crackers:** you are mad

        You're a bloomin maniac: you are mad

        heckers like: (slang) expression of disbelief

97   **stop acting the goat:** stop acting foolishly

98   **mithering:** (dialect) pestering, bothering

99   **Bloomin' hummer!:** (slang) expression of surprise

100   **clout:** hit

        Blimey: expression of surprise, shortened from the saying 'God blind me'

        retire: move back, retreat

101   **supervised care:** looked after by adults

        summat: (slang) something

103   **jumping jack:** a firework that jumps about when lit

        mebbe: (slang) maybe

105   **St Matthew's:** name of a school

107   **chuffed:** pleased

108   **mantelpiece:** ornamental shelf above a fireplace

        paralysed: unable to move

The Mile

111   **report:** written summary of a pupil's school progress

        gammon: a type of ham

        Co-op: grocery shop

        'O' Levels: exams that were taken at the end of Year 11, equivalent to GCSEs

        'A' Levels: advanced level exams taken at the end of Year 13

112   **shrugged:** to draw up the shoulders

        Inattentive: does not pay attention

113   **sarcastic:** cutting, mocking

        don't frame yourself: don't get on with things

114   **St Cuthbert's:** name of a church

        a few bob: about ten pence

The Spanish Inquisition: to be fiercely questioned by someone

he'd been kept down: he had been kept back a year at school

116   **tig:** playground game, tag

lark: mischief, foolishness

you're yeller: you are yellow, you're a coward

Shurrup: (slang) shut up

summat: (slang) something

dirty look: annoyed or aggressive look

120   **cane:** a stick used to hit pupils in schools

121   **poorly:** unwell

tormenting: teasing continually

cornish pastie: pastry filled with meat and potato

122   **pumps:** trainers, plimsoles

124   **spurted:** speeded up

neck and neck: equal, at the same point

The Foursome

127   **Sixteen-inch bottoms:** tight trousers, the narrower at the bottom, the more fashionable

turn-ups: the length of material turned up at the bottom of the trousers

drainpipes: a style of tight trousers

approved school: residential school for young offenders

teddy-boy: a fashion in the 1950s linked to rock and roll music

Borstal: detention centre for young offenders

128   **jessie:** (dialect) unmanly

129   **paisley:** a cone-shaped pattern on material

Slim Jim: a slim tie

Windsor: a type of tie knot

whale-bones: used to stiffen the collar of a shirt

130   **Odeon:** cinema

exhilarating: to feel lively and energetic

Tony Curtis: famous Hollywood actor of the 1950s and 1960s

131 **quiff:** tuft of hair on the forehead, brushed upwards

132 **act the innocent:** to act as if you do not understand

133 **doo-dah:** argument, incident

The Exam

139 **climax:** final or highest point

grammar school: a selective school where pupils had to pass an exam at the end of junior school to gain entry

rehearsal: practice

Napoleonic Wars: wars waged on Europe by Napoleon in the early nineteenth century.

Territorial Army: part-time reserve army made up of civilians

140 **invigilator:** supervisor of an exam

Adam: the first man created by God in the Bible story of Adam and Eve

engrossed: absorbed and involved

141 **commission:** money paid in addition to usual salary, dependent on sales

prospects: expectations, possibilities

fifteen bob: about 75 pence

cadge: borrow

142 **jacked this lot in:** given this up

143 **apprentice:** trainee

144 **condensed milk:** tinned thick sweetened milk

145 **dismissed it:** ignored it as unimportant

146 **white collar worker:** office worker rather than a manual worker who works with his or her hands

Title list

Post-1914 Plays

0 582 30242 0	Absent Friends	Alan Ayckbourn
0 582 06019 2	The Winslow Boy	Terrence Rattigan
0 582 22389 X	P'Tang, Yang, Kipperbang & other TV plays	Jack Rosenthal
0 582 43445 9	Educating Rita	Willy Russell
0 582 08173 4	Shirley Valentine	Willy Russell
0 582 25383 7	Ten Short Plays	
0 582 25394 2	Scenes from Plays	
0 582 06014 1	The Royal Hunt of the Sun	Peter Shaffer
0 582 09712 6	Equus	Peter Shaffer
0 582 06015 X	Pygmalion	Bernard Shaw
0 582 07786 9	Saint Joan	Bernard Shaw
0 582 25396 9	The Rivals/The School for Scandal	Richard Brinsley Sheridan

Post-1914 Stories from other Cultures

0 582 28730 8	Quartet of Stories	
0 582 06011 7	July's People	Nadine Gordimer
0 582 25398 5	Heat and Dust	Ruth Prawer Jhabvala
0 582 07787 7	Cry, the Beloved Country	Alan Paton
0 582 03922 3	Stories from Asia	
0 582 25393 4	Stories from Africa	
0 582 28929 7	Global Tales	

Post-1914 Non-Fiction

0 582 25391 8	Genres
0 582 25384 5	Diaries and Letters
0 582 28932 7	Introducing Media
0 582 25386 1	Travel Writing
0 582 08837 2	Autobiographies
0 582 01736 X	The Diary of Anne Frank

Pre-1914 Fiction

0 582 07720 6	Pride and Prejudice	Jane Austen
0 582 07719 2	Jane Eyre	Charlotte Brontë
0 582 07782 6	Wuthering Heights	Emily Brontë
0 582 07783 4	Great Expectations	Charles Dickens
0 582 28729 4	Oliver Twist	Charles Dickens
0 582 23664 9	A Christmas Carol	Charles Dickens
0 582 23662 2	Silas Marner	George Eliot
0 582 22586 8	The Mayor of Casterbridge	Thomas Hardy
0 582 07788 5	Far from the Madding Crowd	Thomas Hardy
0 582 30244 7	Ethan Frome	Edith Wharton

Pre-1914 Collections

0 582 25405 1	Wessex Tales	Thomas Hardy
0 582 28931 9	Stories Old and New	
0 582 28927 0	War Stories	
0 582 25388 8	Characters from Pre-20th Century Novels	
0 582 25384 5	Diaries and Letters	
0 582 25385 3	Highlights from 19th Century Novels	
0 582 25389 6	Landmarks	
0 582 25386 1	Travel Writing	
0 582 33807 7	19th Century Short Stories of Passion & Mystery	

Pre-1914 Poetry

0 582 22585 X	Poems from Other Centuries

Pre-1914 Plays

0 582 25397 7	She Stoops to Conquer	Oliver Goldsmith
0 582 24948 1	Three Plays	Henrik Ibsen
0 582 25409 4	Doctor Faustus	Christopher Marlowe
0 582 28930 0	Starting Shakespeare	
0 582 43444 0	The Devil's Disciple	Bernard Shaw
0 582 07785 0	Arms and the Man	Bernard Shaw
0 582 28731 6	The Duchess of Malfi	John Webster
0 582 07784 2	The Importance of Being Earnest	Oscar Wilde

NEW CENTURY READERS

Post-1914 Contemporary Fiction

0 582 32847 0	Granny the Pag	Nina Bawden
0 582 29254 9	The Real Plato Jones	Nina Bawden
0 582 25395 0	A Question of Courage	Marjorie Darke
0 582 32845 4	Daughter of the Sea	Berlie Doherty
0 582 43455 6	The Snake Stone	Berlie Doherty
0 582 29262 X	My Family and other Natural Disasters	Josephine Feeney
0 582 31941 2	The Tulip Touch	Anne Fine
0 582 43452 1	Flour Babies	Anne Fine
0 582 29257 3	A Pack of Liars	Anne Fine
0 582 29258 1	The Book of the Banshee	Anne Fine
0 582 29261 1	Madame Doubtfire	Anne Fine
0 582 29251 4	Step by Wicked Step	Anne Fine
0 582 29260 3	Goggle Eyes	Anne Fine
0 582 29255 7	MapHead	Lesley Howarth

0 582 43453 X	A Northern Childhood	George Layton
0 582 32846 2	Lizzie's Leaving	Joan Lingard
0 582 31967 6	Night Fires	Joan Lingard
0 582 43456 4	Goodnight Mister Tom	Michelle Magorian
0 582 43451 3	Journey to Jo'burg	Beverley Naidoo
0 582 36419 1	Aquila	Andrew Norriss
0 582 29256 5	Along a Lonely Road	Catherine Sefton
0 582 46148 0	The Red Pony	John Steinbeck
0 582 31966 8	A Serpent's Tooth	Robert Swindells
0 582 31968 4	Follow a Shadow	Robert Swindells
0 582 31964 1	Urn Burial	Robert Westall

Post-1914 Poetry

| 0 582 25400 0 | Poems 1 | |
| 0 582 22587 6 | Poems in my Earphone | |

Post-1914 Plays

0 582 43450 5	Mirad, a Boy from Bosnia	Ad de Bont
0 582 09556 5	Bill's New Frock	Anne Fine
0 582 09555 7	Collision Course	Nigel Hinton
0 582 09554 9	Maid Marian and her Merry Men	Tony Robinson
0 582 10156 5	The Fwog Prince	Kaye Umansky

Pre-1914

| 0 582 42944 7 | Oliver Twist | Charles Dickens |
| 0 582 29253 0 | Twisters | |